Oscar Sheynin

Recollections and Thoughts in the Twilight of Life

Oscar Sheynin

Recollections and Thoughts in the Twilight of Life

Against the social background

JustFiction Edition

Imprint

Cover image: www.ingimage.com

Publisher:
JustFiction! Edition
is a trademark of
International Book Market Service Ltd., member of OmniScriptum Publishing Group
17 Meldrum Street, Beau Bassin 71504, Mauritius

Printed at: see last page
ISBN: 978-620-0-48913-5

Oscar Sheynin

Recollections and Thoughts in the Twilight of Life

against the social background

Contents

Introduction

To the memory of Ya. G. Rokotov and V. Faibishenko shot at Khrushchev's criminal whim

This is a description of my life shown in a wide context. My narrative is popular and interspersed with short stories and accompanied by a Bibliography. These stories and many inserted details which are hardly known even to my compatriots are interesting in themselves and ensure some insight into the life of my generation. Many authors have dwelt on the horrors of the GULAG; here, the readers will find the much less known dread of living in the Soviet Union at large during the Stalinist period. And I especially focus on the life of my nation.

Notation **S, G**, n means that the source in question is available as a downloadable file n on my website www.sheynin.de which is being diligently copied: Google, Oscar Sheynin, Home

1. Father, Ber (Boris) Abramovich Sheynin

1.1. He graduated from the Vitebsk Commercial School with only the highest marks (also for the Christian God's law) in his certificate and entered the Riga Polytechnic Institute; unlike other Russian educational institutes Jews had been accepted there without constraints.

About 1915 he became the first Russian Jew who obtained a diploma of an assistant locomotive driver. The railway authorities were surprised: a Jewish stoker would be understandable after all, but a assistant driver!

However, after the February 1917 revolution he became able to realize his dream of old and became a cadet of the Petrograd school for preparing officers of the lowest rank (*praporshchiks*) in the Engineering Corps. Indeed, at the end of WWI Jews were allowed to enter military schools. He recited to me and my younger brother a song about the ataman Churkin, no doubt sang by the cadets:

Clouds covered the sky/Fogged are the fields/

So what are you thinking about/Tell us, our ataman.

According to the wish of the majority of cadets (democracy!) although against his own will, father joined them and went to defend the Zimny Palace, the seat of the Provisional Government. There already were a shock battalion, Cossacks and the Women Battalion of Death. The shock battalion had been there almost accidentally, – just boys, hungry and desolate. They scattered, the Cossacks left and the Women refused to meddle in politics.

The cadets were armed with barely anything except rifles and after the salvo from *Aurora* their situation became helpless. All that, but nothing more, was described in a manuscript left by Father. The cadets probably surrendered and some of them including Father went over to the attackers. However, during the battle,

No less than 50 attackers were disabled because of their utter disorder, and I would say, cowardice.

Nevertheless, Father graduated from that school (a group of cadets perhaps graduated with lightning speed). He had a memorable ring on his finger, but later threw it out; it could have costed him his life. A life! Not worth a tuppence. To a large extent Father became an assistant locomotive driver and a cadet to prove (to whom?) that Jews were not inferior to others.

1.2. He became an active participant in the Civil War. In 1919, in Kiev, he commanded a detachment and battled with the Petliura army or perhaps bandits (Petliura allegedly lost control over most of it).

S. P. Petliura (1879 – 1926), writer and journalist, a natural leader who led Ukraine's struggle for independence in 1918 – 1921. Was connected with Jewish pogroms.

Then, as commander of a *bread detachment*, Father sent bread to Kiev from rural areas. Not confiscated but bought the bread which was an exception. Then Father was sent to the Academy of the General Staff, studied there for a year with repeated interruptions for participating in military operations but was dismissed for refusing to attend a talk by Lenin: Why listen to a civilian?

He became chief of reconnaissance in the Defence of the Coast of the Black Sea. In the absence of the Commander received a wire from Trotsky, the head of the Revolutionary War Council: capture the destined for Wrangel twenty seaplanes on board of a French destroyer (or of its auxiliary ship) anchored off the coast of the Black Sea near Odessa. Father succeeded peacefully after protracted talks with the Commander of the destroyer. For a long time he kept the Trotsky wire, but then threw it out: it became extremely dangerous.

Baron P. M. Wrangel (1878 – 1928) was commanding the White army in Southern Russia. Left Russia and was the most prominent White emigre. Probably poisoned by a Soviet agent.

After the war, Father served in military intelligence and Berzin, the assistant head of the Cheka, asked his agreement to become resident spy in Turkey. Muslims are at best not eager to befriend infidels and as a rule they hate Jews, so I do not understand that suggestion. Anyway, Father felt a provocation: agree and be shot! Presumably a mole had been sought out whereas he became acquainted with some top secrets. No, he answered, he would rather continue his education: any future war will be a war of technology and engineers will be badly needed.

1.3. He was indeed sent to the Bauman (later term) Higher Technological School in Moscow. In 1925 – 1931 he, one of the first Soviet graduates, worked in England in Arcos (All-Russian Cooperative Society) as inspector of manufactured machines ordered by the Soviets. Soviet employees had been well paid and, as Mother told me, locals thought that we were only a bit worse off than Americans. The workers of Arcos, but not Father, had been often eating out. I think that as a previous member of the community of military intelligence he was especially cautious. And much later we found out that someone came to Mother's relatives in Vitebsk (!) and asked them about Father. They naturally knew nothing.

Then Father was sent home for participating, during his holidays but without the knowledge of the Consulate, in an international conference in Germany. This punishment was *yet* mild. Refusal to return was impossible: both he and Mother had relatives who held high positions in Moscow. They would have at the very least lost their jobs.

In England, after passing an entrance test, Father became member of the prestigious Institute of Mechanical Engineers, then of the Iron and Steel Institute. That proved sufficient for obtaining, back home, the scientific degree of docent. He never became even a candidate of sciences; how indeed was it possible for him to pass the preliminary examination in Marxist philosophy?

1.4. In Moscow, Father became chief engineer of the Technical Council at the People's Commissariat (Ministry) of Heavy Industry under the head of the all-powerful Ordzhonikidze, member of the notorious Politbureau. It consisted of fifteen or less members and made all the most important government and Party decisions, but gradually became an instrument of Stalin's will.

Father submitted his opinion about industrial projects. Once he criticized one of them, and Ordzhonikidze smilingly suggested: tell that to Stalin since he approved that project.

In 1937 Ordzhonikidze allegedly shot himself or was compelled into suicide or being shot (the Russian Wikipedia now shamefully mentions a heart disease). Indeed, he is known to have had serious disagreements with Stalin. After that Father left his position and had to change several places of work each time unavoidably lowering his status, but avoiding the need to inform on his colleagues. Then someone began to phone him insistently at home. For a few years only members of our family answered the telephone and, upon hearing the familiar but unknown voice, we invariably said *absent*. My explanation of that (comparatively mild) harassment: *Know that Big Brother has not forgotten you.*

Father did not maintain any friendly relations and even fictitiously divorced Mother: otherwise, in case of his arrest she will be labelled *Wife of an enemy of the people*. But most important: he refused to join the Party in spite of a suggestion made apparently in 1931 or 1932 by Lenin's sister Maria Ilyinichna Ulyanova. So how all that told on the health of a man wounded and contused during the Civil War! I think that it was his brother (and my uncle) Mikhail who acquainted him with M. I. Father would have told her some unpleasant facts and she naively thought that such people were needed in the Party. My uncle was an *Old Bolshevik*. He joined the Party being perhaps only sixteen and during the Civil War carried out some dangerous work. I do not know whether he retained his youthful ideals, but he knew how to become acquainted with (Soviet) celebrities. For about ten years he was director of a factory in Moscow.

1.5. One more episode about the Brothers, but first an explanation. Each year all those employed had been obliged to lend *voluntarily* their wages for three or four weeks to the state (*kolkhozniks* who hardly had money were naturally excluded). For ten months the money was being gradually deducted from the wages, then numbered lottery bonds were given out. Drawings lasted twenty years, and a lesser part of the bonds won some money (a very small part won very much) and the rest were redeemed by enormously depreciated money. For some years bonds had been bought by the state for a third of their cost but then this possibility disappeared. There also was the quite free *golden loan* whose bonds had been freely bought back by the state.

In 1947 a currency reform took place. Money in circulation and the bonds of the golden loan lost 9/10 of their value; accounts in the state savings banks lost an essential part but much less than 9/10 although small accounts were left intact.

A person of very high standing divulged those conditions to Uncle who immediately informed Father. Father had bonds of the golden loan but stubbornly did nothing! The network of those on the top! What may we infer about those who were at least a bit higher than Uncle? Even those robbing loans became unprofitable because of their large number and Khrushchev froze the bonds for twenty years. I heard that upon visiting a certain city he saw a room papered by those frozen bonds.

1.6. Back to Father. In 1946, he worked in the Soviet zone of occupation of Germany. Being conferred the rank of lieutenant colonel he inspected the mechanical equipment sent to the Soviet Union in lieu of reparations. By happy chance escaped serious punishment for saving the belongings of a group of Germans from unlawful confiscation; belongings, otherwise certainly remaining mostly in the hands of the local special detachments.

2. The Anglo-American school

2.1. I am six years old and the year is 1931. My parents, I and my brother Leonard (he became Leonid) about a year old have just returned to Moscow. Brother was born in London, duly registered there by Mother and thus became a British-born subject. Then Mother registered his birth in the Consulate and an official there became horrified:

What have you done? He became a British citizen!

Mother excused herself by ignorance.

I came out for a walk in the yard and somewhat older boys encircled me.

Did you see a strike? Do not understand. – *See how the police fought the workers*? I never heard that latter word. – *No, I have not seen*. – *Say: I saw*! – *Yes, I saw*. – *And on whose side were you*?

Well, I have seen policemen (*Bobbies*), all of them tall, in handsome uniforms and even talked to one of them.

On the side of the police. They hit me a bit. – *Say: on the worker's side!* – *On the worker's side*.

They gave me a green twig and let me go in peace.

Father brought over a motorcycle with sidecar, a rarity in Moscow at the time. We also retained a gramophone *His Master's Voice* with a lot of records. One of them was called *Donna Clara* (*Oh, Donna Clara, my arms are waiting for you*). A pretty song but apparently beloved (in German) by wardens of German concentration camps. Another song was sang with a Scot's accent (*togither*) about a Scotsman who was *far across the home* but is returning in a *train that's taking you home, sweet home*! I was unable to find its text in the Internet.

I fell ill. Scarlet fever, complication on the middle left ear, trepanation of the skull. I was in a ward with boys and girls of my age or somewhat younger. A professorial round. *Stand on your beds stark naked*! I think that I understood that in my case that requirement was not needed, but no big deal! So I stood. After the round a girl whose bed was on the other end of our long ward asked me: *Did you see me*? A strange question! I mumbled something and she chirped in a sing-song voice: *I saw you, I saw you*! I had perfectly well understood her perhaps twenty years later when suddenly recollected that episode.

Before being carried downstairs to be moved to the hospital past the flat of Tania Yourgens I eagerly hoped (in vain) to see her … Imagined cutting off the upper layer of her tummy. What for?.. Her father was later arrested and probably shot. Why? Because!

Here is the last episode showing my encounters with girls at that time. I played in our spacious yard with a girl of my age. Then we pissed and I was surprised by her strange habit: she squatted!

2.2. Soon I found myself in the preparatory class of the Anglo-American School. Three such schools were in Moscow: *my*, a French, and a German school, all for the children of the workers of *Comintern*. There were apparently not enough such children for entering *my* school and those speaking some English had been gradually taken on. I did speak although not with ease and even read English. In London, I received my weekly *Chick's Own* and Mother read it to me, but then I somehow began reading it myself (being still unable to read Russian), I only asked Mother about two or three letters.

I think that it was Uncle who managed to join me to *my* school. The Communist International (1919 – 1943) directed the activities of the Communist parties the world over (and largely kept them at the expense of the hungry Soviet Union). Soon, however, it became watched by the Soviet secret service and, from the end of the 1920s, became Stalin's vehicle.

Thus, after the crush of the revolutionary movements of the 1920s in Europe, the unification of the *workers of the world* began anew. Incidentally that slogan about the unification meant that neither nationality, nor religion were important. That was being opposed by each war and to a large extent explained the failure of the Soviet Union.

In London, I attended the junior class of a kindergarten, so my English became well enough for my age. A boy from the senior class was asked a question: add 7 and 5. – *I need an accounting frame*. I had to interfere: 12! I also remember our walk along our street. *Don't step on the cracks* (between flagstones), *otherwise a bear will appear and gobble you up*! That was a warning from a girl, but I asked our teacher whether to believe it. *Oh, I am not sure …*

2.3. In 1935 – 1938 a large part of the workers of Comintern was shot (Courtois et al 1997, chapter 1 of pt. 2) and later it was dissolved following a request of our *cursed allies*. Cominform was created instead (choose between two evils!). Orwell (1945) allegorically and bitingly showed Soviet history. You have not read that book? *Buy, borrow or steal* it. My brother noticed a defect: the pigs had not thought about the world (animal) revolution!

I saw Uncle's accidentally kept letter, apparently written in the 1920s. It ended by the expression *With Communist greetings …* And I also saw a booklet written by him in 1930, *Struggle with the Lack of Roads* in the series *Catch Up* (with) *and Overcome* (the capitalist world). A story: Khrushchev asks a man in the street: *will we catch up and overcome*? *Catch up we will, but not more. Otherwise everyone will see our bare arse.*

But the booklet was fine. Many pictures, one of them naïve: Peasants ask, how much does that Ford cost? References to Party decisions and to two future enemies of the people and a suitable quotation from R. Bacon:

There are three things which make a nation great and prosperous: fertile soil, busy workshops and <u>*easy*</u> *conveyance from place to place.*

Lacking was *a humane political system.*

We had many books published in the 1920s left over from Uncle: during our absence he lived in our flat. Father found them, became indignant and threw all of them away. Later I understood: he was mortally afraid that some books were written by the *enemies of the people*. Yes, such serious danger really existed.

My brother then about seven years old, started to read newspapers and wrote down in a special notebook something about our allegedly suspected Father. Father found that notebook and raised hell. You think that such notes are of no consequence? No, no! It was quite possible to say: *Even a kid suspected something …* Objective proof? *Confession of the accused is the queen of proofs*. That was the notorious Vyshinsky who finally killed himself rather than return on a pretext to Moscow from New York. He thus escaped likely death at the hands of his followers … But if the suspected did not confess? Unimportant. We will get it anyway. And, just in case, give us the man, and a suitable article in the penal code will be found at once and *give the deed the look and sense of law* (Krylov, *The wolf and the lamb*).

Because of our horrible reality Father once remarked about my school: *It would have been better for him to learn how to repair shoes*.

2.4. All the disciplines in our very small school were taught by English and American teachers, naturally in English and at first I did not understand the latter. Russian language was also taught. Our director was Comrade Manevich (and the teachers were also *Comrades*), possibly akin to the eminent Soviet spy Manevich. He was likely from those who (Mikhail Svetlov, translated by Margaret Wettlin)

Went off to fight/With a gun and a pack/

So the poor in Granada/Could get the land back.

We were called by our first names, brought up in the Soviet spirit and sang proper songs, and certainly the Internationale:

Arise, ye prisoners of starvation,/Arise ye wretched of the earth …

The husband of one of our teachers, Libedinsky (not the famous Yu. N. Libedinsky) translated some Soviet songs:

Fly higher, and higher and higher/Our emblem, the Soviet star./

Rot Front! And every propeller is roaring/Defending [?] *the USSR./*

Captain Sir, Captain Sir,/Cheer up, Sir,/

For the sea surrenders only to the brave./

The teacher of Russian organized an amateur performance of Gorky's *Mother* written in 1907 in which I had to say only one line:

They squeeze our blood like juice from huckleberries.

The performance seemed alien to me (and perhaps I envied those who had more to say) and I somehow interchanged *blood* and *juice*.

To my joy, I was dismissed.

I recall a short discussion about the English translation of the Russian omnipresent *ochered*. Our teacher told us: *a line* (stand in line for something) or the Anglicized French word *queue* (main pertinent meaning: *tail*), both rare in everyday English life.

A few times Mother came to our school. Once she spoke with a teacher, but her English was not good enough and the teacher puckered her lips. But Mother suggested to speak French, and so they did, really satisfied with each other. Mother graduated from a gymnasium, attempted to teach me French, but I resisted, as most youngsters certainly (now also) do. Scientific work required the French language and I learned it by correspondence, can read it more or less but nothing more.

While at our school, Mother once called me *Oscar, darling*. Other school students overheard her, and for a long time I remained *Oscar, darling*!

Being already an elderly woman, Mother graduated from the evening department of the Moscow Institute of Foreign languages but was only able to find a teaching job outside Moscow and had been experiencing serious difficulties.

2.5. Among my fellow students some were talented, for example Tibor Szamuely, Ovidius Gorchakov, George Maslov, Dorian Rottenberg (called by someone *Rottenegg*; in translation, he should have chosen the spelling *Rothenberg*).

Our Tibor had the name of his uncle allegedly shot in Hungary. Curtois et al (1997) tell another story, but the important part is this: during the short-lived Hungarian revolution, that uncle, a Jew, was one of the main butchers of the population and played an important role in the later flourishing of anti-Semitism there.

But were Trotsky, the degenerate Kaganovich (whose name on Stalin's decision was given to the Moscow Underground) or Szamuely really Jews? That gang, the *internationalists*, had no nationality at all.

Here is an example of anti-Semitism on the everyday level. Two Israeli sisters owned a house in Berlin, and its inhabitants grumbled: *Jews are sucking our blood.* Then the sisters sold the house to a German, and the grumbling stopped.

Reader, bear in mind: I include many stories without justification, but I am sure that they are at least highly probable. (In a few cases however, I make known about exceptions.) You may still deny them; thus, a British VIP publicly refused to read Solzhenitsyn and apparently denied him, but only to his own disadvantage.

No water in the tap? The Zhids had drank it; There is water? No, it is Zhid's urine.

That was from a long verse of V. Vysotsky, the Russian bard, *The Jews, the Jews encircle us everywhere.* And here is another, possibly imagined story.

A dying old Armenian whispers: *Take care of the Jews* ... His eldest son respectfully remarks: – *Father, we have nothing against them, but why the caring*? – *It will be our turn when they are done with.*

2.6. Stalin at least preferred Azerbaijan to Armenia. Nagorno-Karabach populated almost exclusively by Armenians was given to the preferred Republic, although possibly to *divide and rule*. Unlike most other regions not being Union Republics (not like Russia, Ukraine etc.), it was named according to the geographic rather than ethnic principle.

Was everything bad in the Soviet Union? Certainly not, but what can outbalance many (perhaps even 50 or 60) millions of corpses? Just the same, did free medical care in Nazi Germany outbalance Hitler's butchery?

I am unable to describe Soviet history, but will do all I can although *cannot draw a cart nor eat dry oats* (Shakespeare). Here is a popular song:

Stalin is our military glory,/Stalin is the flight of our youth./

Struggling and conquering with a song,/Our nation follows Stalin./

Stalin can now be replaced by another and subtle dictator.

Yes, we (except those *enemies of the people* and their ilk who perished) followed Stalin and came into a dead end. Followed, how else? Wasn't he infallible and didn't he have divisions aplenty? I refer here to his famous question addressed to Churchill in 1942: *How many divisions the Pope has*? The English Wikipedia tells us that he formulated this same question in 1935 in a conversation with Laval, the French foreign minister.

2.7. But to return to our school. The arrogant Gorchakov became a military spy, then translator of literature into English, but at least Dorian noticed that he had blatantly plagiarized previous translators. Much later he had to meet foreign workers of culture and to explain to them his negative opinion about Pasternak's *Doctor Zhivago*, a forbidden book which he was unable to read either. He also published several papers about the war of 1941 – 1945. I correct my mistake: the story below was written by Vasil Bykov. And so, a guerrilla had to blow up a small bridge guarded on one side of the river by German soldiers. A boy drove up to the bridge and the guerrilla imperceptibly thrusted his small bomb into the boy's cart. The bomb exploded, the bridge was ruined and the boy killed.

Was this morally justified? Listen to Lenin (*Great Sov. Enc.*, third edition, vol. 16, 1974, column 1670; if not stated otherwise, it will always be that edition, also available in English):

Moral is wholly subordinated to the interests of the class struggle of the proletariat.

A statement which recalls the cast of mind of the Jesuits. But the interests of the proletariat rather required the transportation of all the Bolsheviks to the Mo ... No, better to Sirius.

Dorian translated Mayakovsky although some of the selected items were possibly translated previously by foreign translators, but he was afraid to touch even politically barely doubtful authors. During the war he served in a non-combatant unit and I suspect that his psychological condition was not quite normal. Dorian was apprehended while eating swedes in a kolkhoz field and accused of stealing a large quantity of them (a shortfall was discovered). He was morally unable to defend himself, became the scapegoat and sent to a labour camp and his state of mind obviously worsened. He died comparatively early and apparently translated only authors dear to the regime.

George Maslov's mother did time for telling an unsuitable story; George, however, insisted that she was slandered. His father, strange as it was, retained his high position in the Ministry for Foreign Trade. When asked to go abroad for some time he refused to go without his wife. And he it was who obviously set up George in that Ministry and George became there one of its leading workers.

Ellis Buyanovskaya became editor of translations into English and dubbed Russian speech in films into English. She lived in a special house many of whose inhabitants had been arrested. Her elder sister, as I heard, was a lover of Litvinov, a long-standing foreign minister. He was sacked when Stalin became friendly with Hitler; he possibly objected to that alliance and anyway the Germans would have refused to deal with a Jew.

We learned verses from *Hiawatha*:

If you ask me whence these stories,/

Whence these legends and traditions …/

Some years ago I met an American, a teacher of English (British) literature who had not even heard the name of the author of *Hiawatha*, Longfellow. Now I think that he never heard about that epic either. I do not like such narrow specialists. An interesting fact: *Hiawatha* was translated, in particular, into Finnish and Russian, and both translators complained, respectively: English words are too long; too short!

2.8. Our school had a permanent place for a *pioneer camp*. Once I went there. It was a year of starvation which was felt even in Moscow. The camp was situated near Barvikha, almost on the bank of the Moskva River which means: near the place where the people on the very top passed their vacation. After the war Uncle somehow rented a tiny dacha there. He went bathing but the policeman who prevented that stopped him. *Do you know who I am? My name is Sheynin*! The policeman effaced himself. And Uncle told us that the locals grumbled: *Are the ministers' arses cleaner than ours*?

The chief pioneer leader in our camp was named Rappoport. Yes, then it was still possible. One of the boys there, about three years older, spoke perfect English although did not attend our school. His name was Bukharin, so perhaps he was a relative of the great Bukharin (a later enemy of the people).

Once we visited the dacha of a candidate member of the Politbureau Rudzutaks. There, on a lawn, we were shown a real film. We saw two women from his family, but he himself was absent. The *Great Sov. Enc.*, vol. 22, 1975) supplied the year of his death (1938), but shyly passed over in silence that he was shot. *From each according to his ability, to each according to his daily work*!

Usually however I spent summer in Tomilino near Moscow. Uncle together with Father somehow managed to rent it from a city-owned agency; even then it was a feat. There, I made friends with boys of other summer people and met them year after year. We played football, rode bicycles. I had an English *Royal Enfield*, which gradually became small for me but elegant and light. In 1931, people were surprised to see such a beauty.

Neither adults, nor boys ever expressed (then!) any anti-Semitism and I did not even think that I was a Jew. The mother of two boys with whom I regularly met was obviously pleased that her Russian sons were playing with a Jewish boy.

2.9. Our school once more. Tibor's father was arrested and shot about which he wisely kept silent. He himself was imprisoned during the war since he officially called himself a Jew rather than a Hungarian (Hungary was at war with the Soviet Union) and even corrupted his name and became Szamuel.

Tibor was discharged after the leadership of the socialist Hungary petitioned for him. He graduated from the faculty of history of Moscow University, moved to Hungary. Became professor, was sent to some African country. Dorian told me that his colleagues, much inferior to him, had pushed him out. Then Tibor ran away to England, remained professor and actively participated in political life being oriented by his Soviet experience and wrote a few books. In the Soviet Union, they had been kept in special depositories. I only know a title of a booklet of 1969: *Communism and Freedom*. Could have become member of parliament (Dorian's opinion) but died very early.

I exchanged a few e-mails with his daughter, a distinguished journalist and public figure who died as well. Tibor also had a son but I only know (from Dorian?) that he is (was?) a convinced communist. Life is curious!

2.10. I unconsciously turned to mathematics. In literature, I did not even dream of competing with Gorchakov or Joseph Bilik. One of the compositions of the latter began with a phrase *I was born in London in 1686.* He likely recalled Stevenson's *Treasure Island.* In school, we read pieces from that book and were obliged to read it wholly at home. Really to learn English? At first, I had not thought about that and preferred to read Russian books. When being a bit older I decided (why?) that foreign language was not a profession for a man and gradually dropped behind others in English and once to everyone's delight uttered *bibliotion* (library). Only the teacher was disgusted.

History: In a remote century a certain Chinese town on a navigable river began to grow since it was also situated on a caravan route. But why had not that happened a few centuries earlier? No one asked the teacher neither out of shyness did I. For me, history therefore ended (but not anymore!). Then, by the end of my school education I could not even think about machines. Even in London, when Father told me that we were going to have a look at steam locomotives I got afraid and likely wept.

Mathematics, on the other hand, was simple. Prove that the diagonals of a rhombus are mutually perpendicular, and no questions will be asked. And no horrible locomotives. Incidentally, I asked Dorian whether he remembered the formula of the square of the sum of two numbers in English. *No, we have not then got as far as that.* Nevertheless, I remember it well which goes to show that we only remember facts which interest us.

3. The Russian school

3.1. In 1938, all the three special schools were closed probably because Comintern had been decimated. How useful they were! They turned out best specialists in foreign languages. True, we had been very expensive. For example, the standard book of mathematical problems had to be translated for us and published in a tiny run.

And so, each of us went his own way to local schools. Unwillingly I had to learn German, almost the only foreign language taught then.

Wacht auf, verdammte dieser Erde/,
Die stets man noch zum Hungern zwingt!/

That's the Internationale once more. But Heine and Schiller were also studied a bit:

Vor seinem Löwengarten/Das Kampfspiel zu erwarten/
Saß König Franz

(Schiller, *Glove*). Here in Berlin I have once recited these lines to a German woman who was apparently educated according to the German custom, but she never heard them. We also read texts published in Gothic type. I did not like it but later had to read old German scientific literature thus printed, whereas my grandson, who graduated from a German gymnasium, had not seen any such texts.

On the other hand, we had nothing like *Visit to a doctor* or *Shopping*. Soviet citizens did not need the language of everyday life, God forbid!

I arrived in the Russian school in the middle of a school year and, as far as German was concerned, I was a year and a half late. Nevertheless, I managed to *catch up and overcome* others owing to a few private lessons and my English. After moving to Germany I noticed with surprise that my German was a great help.

I recall our able math teacher, Nikolai Gavrilovich Blotsky. When we went over to solid geometry another math teacher had twice given me the lowest mark: I had not (and have not) enough imagination. The corollary of a story about Hilbert: he thought that mathematicians ought to have greater imagination than poets.

3.2. I continue: according to Karl Pearson (1892, p. 15), *The unity of all science consists alone in its method* … Perhaps … *of any given science* … Anyway, it is apparently thought that mathematics consists in the introduction and study of ever more abstract structures which indeed requires imagination!

An article appeared in *Pravda*: school mathematics should be coordinated with life. So our director, Riabov, an easy-tempered and intelligible man who perished in the war, came to inspect our examination in geometry. He asked one of us how to determine the diameter of a round pencil, but had to answer himself: wind a thin wire ten times around the pencil, measure the length of the uncoiled wire etc. But was this problem so important? I myself was asked once: how to measure the volume of a haystack? I do not remember the correct answer, but a haystack is certainly not a truncated pyramid.

Physics: I was unable to understand electricity. Our teacher had not told us that, after all, physics is an experimental science, and proofs (if possible) had not been discovered by means of school mathematics. (Composition of forces which belongs to school physics is only experimentally justified.) Chemistry remained alien, I had no interest in its subject. Our biology teacher was not really qualified and we did not take her seriously. Geography, history? As taught, mostly consisted of collections of facts and did not therefore represent science.

I wrote grammatically rather correct, but was too young to feel, for example, the beauty of the generally known Tatiana's letter to Onegin. And I had not understood the first lines of *Eugene Onegin*; here is their literal translation:

My uncle kept to most honest rules. […]

He compelled us to respect him.

But how did he compel *us*? A few decades later I heard an explanation (rejected by some specialists): in those times, it meant that uncle had died. Literature, however, was mostly applied to rear us ideologically.

In the ninth (the last but one) class we had to study *military matters.* If I am not mistaken, the girls were taught how to render first aid and we, boys, were given some practical information, for example, how to orient ourselves by Sun and watch. Mainly, however, we had apparently been psychologically prepared for military service.

An order of a superior is the law for the subordinates since it represents the will of the nation!

And a supplied addition: Previously, there was a reservation: … *except wrecking orders* … It was deleted since soldiers had been refusing to obey dangerous orders. I myself add: except irrelevant orders.

4. The war is approaching. Its beginning

4.1. Germany with Hitler at its head suddenly became our ally. Some discussion of that spectacular event took place in our class. Vitya Mitelikov, a future officer in the fleet, remarked that *they oppress Jews*. Our class teacher hesitantly answered: *Perhaps that changed.* Changed indeed, but little did we know.

A story: Why do the Germans concentrate their armed forces on our border? To escape (British) *air raids. And why we are doing the same? To protect them.*

With two or three friends I visited an Officers' House (a later term). We saw a great wall map of Europe and one of my friends asked me whether I lived anywhere except London. An officer went by and remarked:

You are looking at the wrong place. The Germans have just occupied Belgrade.

And I thought: *So what*? That was in April 1941. The Soviet Union had just concluded a mutual aid pact with Yugoslavia but the pocket Supreme Soviet had not yet ratified it. Had Stalin wished to interfere, such trifles would not have stopped him.

At least a few reliable and knowledgeable people had warned Stalin about the impending attack, but he never trusted anyone. One of those people was Churchill, another one was Sorge, a Soviet spy in Japan. Sorge was later apprehended and the Japanese had been prepared to trade him for someone of their own (spies?). This had not happened and Sorge was hanged. So why was not he exchanged?

It was strongly suspected that Stalin did not wish to see a living witness of his criminal obstinacy of refusing to recognize the imminent danger. A Japanese source reported that in 1937 Sorge disobeyed an order to return to Moscow and thus escaped a likely execution: Stalin's feverish imagination saw great many people on the top as traitors hiding under the bed. A German author whose name I forgot remarked that, had *The Damned* (as Solzhenitsyn called him) been replaced by a German spy, the damage to the nation would not be as great. In 1964, long after Stalin's death, Sorge posthumously became Hero of the Soviet Union.

According to another source, Sorge told the Japanese everything he knew in return for a (kept) promise to leave alone a few women who were somehow connected with him. But still, his merits were enormous and he should have been exchanged. Indeed, he also reported in 1942 that Japan will not declare war, and troops from Siberia were sent to defend Moscow.

One of the craziest sentences was meted out by the Soviets *after the beginning of the war* to an official for predicting it during the alliance of the two countries.

After Hitler's accession war became imminent (as foreseen by Stalin, see below). Neither England, nor France, being democratic countries, was able to prepare itself properly and many of their political leaders just did not realize the danger; Churchill was a rare exception, but he was not yet important. Edward VIII of the United Kingdom was, in plain words, Hitler's enthusiastic spy. In 1936, luckily for the world, he abdicated for romantic reasons.

A pact between those two countries and the Soviet Union had failed to materialize. To participate in the war Soviet troops would have to cross Poland, but Poles refused to allow the Stalin *billy goat into their kitchen garden* (a Russian saying). Anyway, Poland, situated between two cut-throat bandits and lacking real help from the West, was doomed. Each of the three other nations began to make advances to Germany and the Soviets succeeded.

4.2. Should we be surprised at the predilections of Edward VIII? One of the grandsons of the present Queen of the United Kingdom arrived at a fancy dress party clad in a uniform of a Nazi storm trooper. Was (is) he so stupid? Certainly not, but classically educated: Aristotle, Shakespeare … But Hitler, Stalin? Not comme il faut! And for France and Spain just replace Shakespeare by Molière and Cervantes respectively. After the Soviets had invaded Afghanistan the American embassy discovered that no one there spoke Russian. Ignorance of everyday events is amazing. Too many people on the very top are blind to the great danger of militant Islam.

It is high time for those responsible and for public figures to realize that from the social-political viewpoint the extremely influential militant Muslims constitute a special subspecies of *homo sapiens*, the *homo assassinus* (killer).

A large number of German Jews had managed to escape abroad but experienced great difficulties when attempting to settle somewhere. Some, including celebrated scientists, came to the Soviet Union but many of them landed in GULAG. Why? Because they were infected with democratic notions, and will spread their pestilential views over our honest defenceless population.

A German family arrived in Tomilino. Their boy, a youngster aged about seventeen, began working as a postman and had to carry moderate sums of money. He told some boys of the summer people, me included, that he was attacked by someone but managed to escape practically unharmed. The youngster did not comment at all and I had a strong impression that the attacker was not a petty criminal.

The governments of many countries just did not understand their national interests and refused entry to those Jews whereas Jewish organizations there had hardly interfered, even the horrible Crystal Night did not help. They, just as their governments had been afraid of additional unemployment and a burst of anti-Semitism. The Australian representative at the League of Nations declared that his government (short-sightedly) wished to remain purely Christian, as though Chinese and Japanese newcomers had not rather soon been admitted.

Poor Hitler being additionally influenced by the Arabs who protested against Jewish return to their historical homeland, was simply forced to adopt somewhat stricter measures …

We have always been pawns on the world scene. During WWII England and US knew the location of the German extermination camps perfectly well, but had not dropped a single bomb on them. Why? The oil?

4.3. The war began and air-raid warnings were heard in Moscow but at first no bombing had occurred.

Arise for the mortal battle,/Arise, ye willing people,/ …

The poet who composed that song, which became generally known, was accused (perhaps posthumously) of plagiarism. The widow of an officer who perished in WWI allegedly gave him its text (for publication but certainly not under his own name), and he only replaced *German* by *fascist*.

The telephones of almost every Moscow (only Moscow?) citizen were disconnected, only people very important for the regime and the *servants of the people* were excluded. A story about questions asked by a foreigner:

That crowd … Who are those people? – The people. – And who rides in the cars over there? – Their servants.

We had to store our radio receivers (which just became available) in local post offices. No need to hear Hitler! No pertinent official document had ever appeared, and I only saw a signed (not editorial) article in *Izvestia*: *some irresponsible citizen had not yet given away their receivers* … Money from deposits was only allowed to be drawn in small amounts. Father's motorcycle was requisitioned.

About 1950 one of those whose telephone was not disconnected published an article in *Izvestia*. Telephone calls, don't you see, are disturbing him. I wrote a letter to the newspaper, recalled a classical operetta. A middle-aged woman tells her young niece:

Now that you are getting married, I may reveal a frightful secret: At night, men are snoring, and this is awful. ... But it is much worse if you do not hear such snoring …

The newspaper's answer was of no consequence. And here is a sudden ending of this theme. My wife told me once:

Had not the telephone in my (communal) *flat been taken out of service, I would have married long before meeting you.*

So how many girls remained single or married late, or married almost anyone? But who cared?

To explain the great losses in the beginning of the war Stalin invented a fable about the action of permanent and temporary factors. German invasion was sudden (a blatant lie!), their victories and the occupation of vast territories were temporary etc. Understandably, neither the Russian Wikipedia, nor the third edition of the *Great Sov. Enc.* had mentioned those factors. In the early 1970s I read an article in *Izvestia* or *Pravda* about which I only remember that the author was a marshal and that he ridiculed those factors.

The Red Army sometimes retreated in a horrible disorder A cadet of the Odessa Artillery School described to a few fellow cadets, me included (§ 6), how he in a group of soldiers went East on a lorry with bags of paper money. I forgot wherefrom was that money, but recall that those soldiers were unable to find an official prepared to sign for it. So they burned the money although each took a roll for himself. That cadet deposited his money in a (state-owned) savings bank and very soon a *political instructor* asked him about its provenance. *Sold my hut*. The Soviets forestalled contemporary efforts to curb money laundering.

4.4. Practically all Jews who had been living and remained in the occupied territories perished. Evacuation was impossible since too frequently the army retreated with lightning speed whereas transportation was anyway insufficient. But there was another circumstance. A great majority of the population, of the army officers, of the Jews themselves knew nothing about the Nazi atrocities. Ignorance was amazing. Uncle told us that, in October 1941, when Moscow was all but captured, some people including him were selected for underground activities in the city. Him, whose Jewishness was recognisable from afar!

Yes, all but captured. I read somewhere that a plane with a highly esteemed ikon flew around Moscow. Only Stalin could have ordered such a flight. In his youth he was expelled from a seminary allegedly for propagandizing local (Tiflis, then Tbilisi) workers but actually, as I heard, for frequenting bordellos. The Leninist – Stalinist bestial persecution of religion surely meant that the army was never informed about the flight and that the pilot hardly lived more than a few days after it. But this tells us about Stalin's hidden feelings about religion.

My sister once removed and her husband ran away from Riga. He told me that he had been working alongside a polite German with a Nazi badge (that's a German for you!). The father of my sister, an educated man, refused to leave and perished together with wife and son (with my aunt and cousin). That man recalled the kind Germans of old.

My cousin managed to board a train with Riga Jews. They reached a certain town, but the Soviet railway commandant prevented their farther journey: military evacuation was of paramount importance. The Jews ignorantly went back …

The fate of the Bessarabia Jews was different. Stalin planned to begin to attack Germany from there also, and, prior to that never occurred attack, on the night of 14 June 1941, all local Jews were evacuated in goods wagons to remote regions of Siberia. They were given half an hour to prepare themselves, but why such a hurry? One more example of foolish and quite unnecessary cruelty. Many of those Jews perished.

4.5. During the cold war the *enemy voices* (radio broadcasts from leading Western nations and, in the first place, from radio *Freedom*) read out (to those of us who had been hearing them in spite of the fierce jamming) passages from *Aquarium* by Suvorov, a deserter from the Main Intelligence Agency of the army. He described unknown to us facts, his style was extremely peculiar and effective, and I believed him. It occurred that the Soviet armed forces in the Western regions of the country had been wholly prepared for a sudden occupation of continental Europe, so that all the officers there (and partly the soldiers) should have been in the know. Then, however, it became known that Suvorov had corrupted some facts about his personal life abroad as a spy (and not in Austria but in Switzerland).

The jamming went on mercilessly and had cost a pretty penny, but who cared?

The Marxist – Leninist ideology is opposed to the bourgeois ideology and uncompromisingly struggles with it (*Great Sov. Enc.*, vol. 10, 1972, column 108). But was this relevant to the case described above?

Are you listening to enemy voices? Don't you have a radio (with a single programme; later, with three programmes)? *Aren't you able to read Pravda, or at worst, Izvestia? There are no izvestia (information) in Pravda and no pravda (truth) in Izvestia? So you wish to settle in northern Siberia, the rotten intellectual that you are*?

Then I read Suvorov's *Icebreaker* and disagreed with much. Why had he apologized to his father? He revealed essentially important historical facts. First, the indirect help rendered by Stalin to Hitler by demanding German communists to oppose mainly, in the forthcoming elections of 1933, the social-democrats. He correctly thought that Hitler, once he becomes Reichskanzler, will be an icebreaker and start a great war in Europe so that he, Stalin, will be able to intervene at the right moment. Second, Stalin himself had intended to attack Germany but was late by about a fortnight.

Nevertheless, Suvorov's narrative was defective. He could have shortened it by about a half, and his arguments were not always thought out properly. Thus, the appearance of a Soviet tank supplied by both tracks and wheels was not an indication of that intention: upon reaching European roads, and especially German autobahns on tracks, the tank will indeed abandon them and speed along on wheels. But would wheels seriously hinder the tank from participating, at first, in defensive battles?

4.6. Generally known was Stalin's statement of 1940:

On each and every attack our valorous Red Army will answer with three blows. We will fight on foreign soil and achieve victory with small losses.

Forgotten was the saying: *Chicks should be counted in autumn*, in the autumn of 1941.

Block (poem *Twelve*) had properly declared:

To get the bourgeoisie/We'll start a fire,/

A worldwide fire/And drench it with blood/ …

Yes, we started a fire, barely escaped with heaviest losses. But Stalin, the great military leader, became generalissimo. *The Great Sov. Enc.* listed people thus honoured including Suvorov, 1729 or 1730 – 1800 (about whom serious reservations were published abroad), but missed two of them, Franco and Chang Kai-Shek. Franco, whom the Soviets labelled as a fascist, was greatly meritorious: in spite of Hitler's insistent demands, he refused German troops a passage across Spain for capturing Gibraltar, and thus for saving the German great army in Africa from imminent ruin (comparable with the Stalingrad defeat).

But then, had not the Soviets realized that it was possible to preventively deliver the *three blows*? Suvorov's book was reasonable but he drew upon himself the rage of many Soviet citizens including his own father (see above).

5. Chelyabinsk

5.1. For five days Mother with me and my brother travelled to Chelyabinsk in a freight train. Some families of the employees of the *Narkomat* (Ministry) in which Father had been working were evacuated to that city and he himself joined us in a few months.

We were expected. The three of us were housed in a nice flat on (yes, you guessed correctly!) *Stalin street*, but the second of its two rooms was given over to another family. I recall an episode. Winter, snow, wind … Many people gathered at the tramway terminal, waiting and shivering. And here comes *the proper* tram which passes our house. It is immediately packed by lucky passengers, but then an announcement is heard: change of route! We all go out and a single man enters! Two people came up to him, to the chief of the tramway service, to a *servant of the people*: *We will lodge a complaint*! Others remained passively in the cold and I mentally kicked him out.

There, in Chelyabinsk, I had attended the last (the tenth) class of school and graduated from it. I remember how inequalities began to be studied. I attempted to replace them by equations with a correction term but now I think that equalities and inequalities should be studied at the same time.

5.2. In Moscow, after many years, I came across one of my fellow school students, Tania Gnedina, a daughter of an eminent and repressed journalist. She became a physicist, compiled a biography of Einstein and gave her manuscript to a (certainly state-owned) publishing house. It was rejected: *Your Einstein is a Zionist*! The Party approved refutations of the theory of relativity, a theory of a Jewish idol.

Marchuk, the President of the Academy of Sciences, supported Logunov, the main refuter of that theory. In 1974 – 1991 the know-all Logunov had been vice-president of the Academy … There was, however, a period of sensibility: in 1955 (*Great Sov. Enc.*, second edition, vol. 31) that theory was found to agree with dialectical materialism. And, when describing relativity theory, the third edition of that source (vol. 18, 1974, pp. 623 – 628) did not mention philosophy at all. So how did Logunov feel himself?

The Moscow bigwigs lagged far behind their former German counterparts. In 1936, the journal *Deutsche Mathematik* (a suitable title for Nazi Germany!) published a letter *from a student* who (Sheynin 2003a, p. 136) called the work of the great physicist

A declaration of war for the extermination of the Nordic-Germanic feeling of nature,

i. e., for the extermination of common-sense mathematics. Such atavism after Riemann and Hilbert (not Jews at all)! But common sense certainly remains, at least during initial studies.

5.3. My just mentioned paper included the text of a (German) manuscript written by Mises, *Mathematics and the Third Reich* which I had discovered. It was signed by letters R. S., *Roh Stoff* (raw material) in my interpretation.

I hoped to receive useful comments from Siegmund-Schultze, a known German historian of mathematics, but he bristled up: *Rohstoff* is a single word (a professor of mathematics in Cologne told me that in my instance that was unnecessary) so that the authorship of the manuscript remains unknown, that he saw the manuscript many years ago and that in general I should leave Mises to Germans and stick to Russian mathematics since my paper (1998a) was fine.

He saw the manuscript but did not publish it because of its strange signature. So I had not surrendered to that insolent fellow (who recently became co-editor of *Historia Mathematica*).

Mises was a Jew. In 1934 he freely moved to Turkey, lectured there in French, then moved to the US. There is literature aplenty about science in Nazi Germany; as far as mathematics is concerned, the best book is perhaps Segal (2003 and 2004). Here is an episode (end of 1933 or beginning of 1934).

The Minister of Higher Education visited Göttingen and asked Hilbert whether the level of the university lowered after the expulsion of the Jews. *Lowered? The university does not exist anymore*! I was unable to find a reference to a witness of that episode.

Göttingen was the world mathematical centre, nowadays that centre is likely in the US.

5.4. In Chelyabinsk, I had time to attend for one term the local Institute for Mechanization of Agriculture. The chair of mathematics was Professor Yuriy Yurievich Nut (Nutt?), an Esthonian who graduated in Petersburg, a deputy of the Supreme Soviet of the Esthonian Republic. Garshnek (Harshnek), one of his few Esthonian postgraduates, conducted our classes.

Nut lectured splendidly, I attended them open-mouthed. He examined me, I got full marks and he remarked that my proper place was in a university.

Descriptive geometry began with a theorem: *a projection of a point is a point.* I had not taken this discipline in earnest, then suddenly and much too lately changed my mind. Just before the examination someone of us hid a few of the unpleasant models of the intersection of geometric bodies.

Physics, still methodologically difficult for me. English. I said a few words which was more than enough, and the same always happened in my future examinations. The only exception occurred at the candidate examination (prior to the defence of my candidate dissertation). My grammar was hardly in existence which was forgiven, but then I had to translate orally about ten pages of a printed English text. I translated about five and refused to continue and my decision was approved by the appropriate chair.

While about it, I also mention that there were two more candidate examinations. Marxist philosophy: I only just managed to get the least possible positive mark, although as a student of the geodetic institute
(§ 9) I diligently studied Marx, attempted to discover essential truths. Now I think that he only formulated principles rather than working propositions. Thus, the celebrated principle *Freedom of a person ends at the point in which begins the freedom of another person* is practically useless.

Finally, the examination in mathematics. It proved very difficult for me, but I got through.

6. The artillery school

6.1. I was drafted into the army. A fellow student remarked: *I thought that Jews do not serve in the army*. There are many documents showing Jewish participation in the *Great Patriotic War*, as it is officially called; see also § 13.2; in § 6.2 I mention a named pistol awarded to a Jew. My boyhood friend, *Willy* Hershenson was killed as were quite a few other Jewish boys from our large apartment house.

And so, through the efforts of Uncle (after whom my son was named) I found myself in the privileged Frunze Odessa High-Calibre Artillery School (rather than in a university). It was evacuated to Sukhoi Log, a small town situated between Sverdlovsk and Chelyabinsk. Frunze was a military commander, held highest military and party positions, evidently became too independent. Beloved by the military since he forbade *commissars* to meddle in military decisions, he died during an unnecessary operation which the Damned forced upon him (and orchestrated?). Kotovsky, Chapaev, Shchors, heroes of the civil war, became either too independent or too beloved by the army, and all three perished. What an accidental case!

We had the most powerful mobile howitzers of the calibre of 152 and 203 *mm* (6 and 8 inches), but I was sent to the battalion (not to be understood in the more common sense) of artillery instrumental reconnaissance, topography battery. Our platoon (as also a few other platoons in the battalion) consisted almost entirely of graduates of one of the Moscow artillery secondary schools. While in formation, they sang artillery, curious lyric or barely understandable songs (I also when learned them):

Command will come,/Command will come,/
No extra word we'll hear,/[...] */We'll smash the targets,/*
/All the targets,/With misses none,/With misses none./

Tania, Tanuisha, Tatiana, my dear!/
Hot was that summer, still hotter our love,/
We shouldn't, we cannot forget it, my dear!
(From a Russian chanson *Siniy Beret*, *Blue Beret.*)

Bathing went Veverley, Veverley,/
Back home Dorotheya is left./
Swimming he didn't, really unable,/
So takes two buoys of sorts./
(From a student song of old.)

6.2. I recall Sinitsin, son of a Party functionary, honest believer in the Soviet way of life; Andreev, son of some police chief. He became our *court photographer*, always came as such, never in formation, to all the reviews. Then, Alferiev, son of a general reported missing in action. Near the end of the war another general, a friend of his father told the wife: likely killed; had he been captured, even under a false name, the Germans would have recognized him and trumpeted their success to the world.

Eremin, likely commander-born. I recall the obscene verse which he recited:
No, I cannot, I'm unable./Yes you can, I'm sure you will!/
Down I bend, and you will enter.

I think that they all had lived worthily and hope that some of them are still alive. And I especially recall Beloskursky and regret very much that I had not met him anymore. Son of a general, polite and modest.

There also was, in another platoon, Kleonsky, a Jew and electrical engineer. Psychologically unfit for military service, and possibly not quite healthy. I myself got readily tired and sleepy, but found out the reason only after becoming a civilian: low blood pressure. I do not remember whether it was measured at the drafting, but anyway it was not as low as to make any difference. Had not Kleonsky's condition the same cause? He wounded himself intentionally by an allegedly faulty carbine and disappeared.

For some time the *starshina* (sergeant major) of one of the batteries was Bun, a Jew and a previous front line sniper. About 1950 I came across him in Moscow but he died very soon. He told me that he was not a usual sniper but a graduate of a school of *sniping* and was awarded a named pistol which he gave away to the commander of his battery. Was this act the reason why he became sergeant major? As a civilian, he repaired domestic refrigerators. His Jewish wife, a teacher of foreign languages, was jobless – not surprisingly.

Officers at the artillery school called us *you* rather than (the not at all dated Russian) *thou* or *Comrade cadet*. No anti-Semitism at all, everything on the pre-war level. And, on the same level, in a routine order: *Write off a cartridge spent by ... while on sentry duty at ...*
(At night, he fired in the air to scare off a stray cow.)

The chief of the utility service was lieutenant Berkovich. Numerous stories were told about him. Now I think that he himself spread most of them to confirm his known harmlessness. Here is one. Berkovich tells the officer on duty: *For today, I need a horse* [with cart] *or two cadets.* And indeed, we often had to work hard on various occasions (and peel potatoes).

While guarding a food store cadets of another platoon of graduates of a secondary artillery school stole a lot of food, hid it somewhere in the barracks, and began to consume it day after day in addition to the usual ration. Their store was accidently discovered and uproar followed. The entire platoon found itself in the guardroom, all the sergeants in such platoons were dismissed and possibly degraded (I do not remember that) and new sergeants were selected for us from cadets of the *usual* platoons. No further steps were however taken (the *clever* platoon was freed) so apparently the whole business was hushed up.

6.3. Our teachers were honestly working and knowledgeable officers. The subjects were topography, artillery, tactics and we were certainly politically instructed. We studied the measurement of angles by simple theodolites, the laying out and calculation of traverses, exploratory surveying during which distances are measured by pairs (and even triads) of steps. Reader! Try such measurements out for yourself, only without fail walk in your usual manner.

Double steps measure the distance/In the field, in the open.

This verse was certainly copied from a soldier song of old:

Falcons, soar like eagles,/Sorrows, time to leave alone,/

Under canvas better camp/In the field, in the open.

Artillery (Captain Alekseenko): I recall the long ago abandoned preliminary firing with observation of short falls and shots over. Being at the observation post (OP), determine the distance and direction of firing for the guns which are not on the straight line target – OP at all. And, after sighting each hit-point, correct both parameters by approximations. We had to accomplish all this (somehow fictitiously invented) on paper, almost in no time.

The most serious was the mutual orienting of several batteries. They had to observe simultaneously an air benchmark (a burst of a shell). In principle, this was similar to the determination of the longitudinal difference between two points by simultaneously observing a celestial event (e. g., a lunar eclipse) from both.

Tactics. Our instructor, Captain Bochkarev, read out to us an enthusiastic newspaper article about a gun-layer of high-calibre guns. Alone unhurt, he carried the heavy shells, loaded a gun and fired, so what will you say? We agreed with the author, but Bochkarev corrected us: trenches should be dug out as soon as possible for protecting the crew of the guns. What rate of fire can a single man achieve?

Drills: really difficult for me. Bayonet combat (long ago forgotten): *thrust from afar, thrust when near*! Service regulations: see end of
§ 3.2.

Political instruction: we made fun of an instructor and a cadet told us a story (possibly true) about a political instructor who allegedly searched the ground for a lost point of zero. A written confession of a wounded political instructor was read to us. He alone remained on the OP alive and unwounded, saw that German tanks were just about reaching an important bridge and ordered the commander of the guns by field telephone: *Shoot at the enemies of the revolution*! (Revolution indeed!) And the answer: give me the distance, the direction, you SOB! He bitterly repented of his ignorance. In Bulgaria, however, in an artillery brigade (§ 7.2), the soldiers certainly respected their (Jewish) political instructor.

A quarter-master-sergeant was discovered as gone AWOL for a long time. Court-martial:

Why did you go AWOL? – What else could I do? Masturbate?
He was sent to a penal company (and to an almost certain death) and I doubt that repentance would have softened that verdict.

All our quarter-master-sergeants were unfit for active military service, so was it allowed to send that poor devil to a penal company?

A colonel replaced the commander of our school, a general, and began to tighten the screws. This did not however concern us, the cadets. But then he noticed another poor devil smoking near the formation which just then sang the brand new national anthem (*Unbreakable union of freeborn republics* …). But why wasn't he in the formation? Penal company, incomparable cruelty.

6.4. Our cadet ranks, and those of our instructors began to be filled by front line soldiers/officers. They saw the elephant and felt the Soviet military reality on their own backs. Anti-Semitism appeared. Solzhenitsyn (2001 – 2002) explained: relatively more Jews were (understandably!) more noticeable in headquarters, among senior officers, military physicians etc. than in the front line. A story: an inspecting military bigwig suddenly sees a Jew in the front line:

And what are you doing here? – Escaping mobilization!

In the beginning of 1945 out school returned to Odessa, to its previous enclosed block. With the howitzers and everything else, even firewood, stored in waggons rather than in open platforms (therefore hidden since forbidden to move so as to save coal). The return, on several special trains, lasted a few months, so how was it allowed during the war? No classes were held for some time even in Odessa.

Prisoners of war were housed in our block as well. They worked somewhere and one of them repaired my watch. The commander of our battery asked another German to regulate our *burzhuika* (a small iron oven placed in a room), and I interpreted: – *Macht viel Kohl in die* [in der] *Luft* (Makes much cabbage in the air). – *Raucht*? (Smokes?) *Yes, yes*! In German, *cabbage* and *coal* are pronounced and written similarly.

I saw a small formation (not well kept) of soldiers clad in strange uniforms lacking shoulder straps. They passed our school along an adjacent street, an escorting soldier with a carbine with them. And suddenly a few cigarette packages fell to my feet. So they were repatriated soldiers and thus they had greeted me. Repatriated meant freed by our allies and therefore all the more suspicious. Many of them (relatively much more, as I imagine, than of those freed by us) landed in the GULAG. *The Germans are holding only traitors, but not prisoners of war*! Several millions of traitors. That was the incontestable declaration of the Damned whereas Americans decorated their military men who became prisoners of war by a special medal.

In the beginning of the war many soldiers and some officers went over to the Germans because they had suffered much more than enough under the Stalinist regime, so who was the real traitor? A cadet told me about a German leaflet: *Come over but do not forget spoon or greatcoat*!

I cried: *I do not smoke. – Give them away*. But nothing was left, passers-by promptly picked up the packages. When being about twelve years old I lighted a cigarette and inhaled a few times. It was very pleasant and I decided that smoking was too dangerous: quitting would be impossible. Cf. Mark Twain:

There is nothing easier than quitting. I myself have done it 27 times.

6.5. A reference was prepared for each of the graduating cadets. It contained a decisive phrase: *Devoted to the Lenin – Stalin party*. For some of us, but not for me, that statement was more definite: *Deeply devoted* … I did not at once understand that that unofficial name was intended to glorify Stalin once more.

For a few days I roamed the streets of Odessa clad in uniform with shoulder straps of a junior lieutenant. I talked with a few American sailors from a merchant ship. They told me:

You speak good English. Save money and come to us.

I, a newly-fledged officer, did not like their advice. And they were certainly naïve, but what can you expect from American sailors? I also spoke with two sailors from a European ship. We walked a few minutes, came to a restaurant and they entered. I had no such intention, and just then an officer patrol stopped me.

You are not supposed to walk about with foreigners. – No, no, I just showed them the way.

7. Bulgaria

7.1. I graduated in April 1945 and, together with most of the graduates was held in reserve in Gorokhovetsky camps. I remained there for a few months. It was cold, damply and awfully dull. Some *chemists*, as we called them, were quartered near us. They, a military unit, remained there all through the war, just in case.

Then I was sent to Bulgaria. Travelled through Odessa, visited my school, but everything seemed to me somehow changed. A woman in the street asked me, an officer in uniform, what do I sell. That's Odessa for you.

In Sofia, there was a Tsar-Liberator Boulevard. During the rule of Tsar Aleksandr II the Liberator, serfdom in Russia was abolished and Bulgaria liberated from the Turks mostly by Russian troops. Incidentally, among those troops was a Jewish regiment, rather soon disbanded. And in 1944 or early 1945 that boulevard was renamed after Tolbukhin, marshal and commander-in-chief of the Southern Group of (Soviet) Forces. Later the previous name of the boulevard was restored. Similarly, Burgas, one of the main Bulgarian cities, a Black Sea port, was renamed after Stalin, but later its previous name was restored. I recall a caricature in a Bulgarian (?) newspaper of ca. 1960: Stalin is looking down from the sky at that previous name Burgas, written on a map with *Stalin* crossed out, and decides: they had changed their alphabet.

7.2. In Bulgaria, in a Guard artillery brigade, I became commander of a platoon of topographic reconnaissance. Our barracks were in Plovdiv, a most important city. Near us there was a settlement named after Stolypin, and there, while on duty, I, with two or three soldiers, entered an Orthodox church. In the Soviet Union, such liberties had only been possible for old men and those of humble social status. The same was certainly true for the Jews and synagogues.

An instructor of the Moscow Geodetic Institute and a Party member was reprimanded for such a visit; he was on duty of sorts and freezing. After the service the priest came up to us and thanked the soldiers for coming, but as though (understandably) did not notice me.

In the central part of Plovdiv Turkish bootboys called up Soviet military: *Cleaning, cleaning, we're Moscow specialists.* For a small remuneration they offered to smear their faces with shoe polish.

I began to read Bulgarian newspapers and even read the Bulgarian translation of *Crime and Punishment*. I had not read it in Russian, understood the text in general less many details. Memorised a few Bulgarian verses:

The years went by but I forgot you not;

When in need of fresh foodstuffs, come to the shop of Uncle Mitko.

About a year ago, in 2017, I recited the latter to a doctor, a Bulgarian, and he laughed heartily. Many words were almost the same as in Russian. Thus, *zhivot* (belly) meant *life*, just like in Church Slavonic and in a Russian saying. Some words were borrowed from English and French (and surely German). Thus, *shop* became *shopa* and *camion* remained *lorry*.

In 1957, being a geodetic engineer, I translated a Bulgarian book by Hristov (1946). He visited Moscow and went with me to Sudakov, head of the Directorate of Geodesy and Cartography. I only had to translate a single word: Hristov did not understand the Russian *Eyler* (Euler). But then he improperly asked me to wait outside since he intended to have a special talk with Sudakov. Improperly, because he did not warn me beforehand.

Hristov was head of Laboratory of geodesy (these words do not really agree with each other) at the (Bulgarian) Academy of Sciences. A Committee on geodesy and geophysics was established in the Soviet academy in 1955.

7.3. The general situation in the army seemed strange. The war was over, but demobilization had only begun about half a year later and was essentially restricted. It only concerned much older soldiers, miners and agronomists. It became gradually clear that Stalin planned to capture continental Europe and apparently only an exceptionally bad harvest prevented such attempts. Soldiers had not questioned me about the situation and I remained silent. Lieutenant Serkov, a much older geodetic engineer, lean and nimble-footed, was also demobbed. Soldiers much respected him, and he kissed good bye to each of them in our battery.

Service in such times is morally difficult. Sergeant Drosdov went weekly to some musical rehearsals which were allowed by the commander of the brigade. I asked him whether he really wished to participate. – *Without them I would have hanged myself.*

I fell ill after a cold: paralysis of the facial nerve, my face became distorted.

8. Germany

8.1. I was more or less cured in a hospital, and then Father, a lieutenant colonel in East Germany (§ 1.6), became able to transfer me there, to the Group of the (Soviet) Forces in Germany. However, I found myself in a hospital in Potsdam where my health was finally restored although the paralysis had recurred two or three times.

A German masseur came regularly to treat a patient in our ward (and perhaps other patients elsewhere) and the patient fed him up. In Berlin, German physicians were forbidden to treat Soviet citizens.

I suddenly met my maternal uncle Yakov, an eye doctor, a Major of medical service, who worked in that same hospital. He had to select glasses for highest officers and once for a German high-ranking officer accused of war crimes. While being arrested, he was unable to take his glasses and therefore refused to read the indictment. Uncle was asked to select glasses for him and promised help of an interpreter. However, uncle did not need any such help.

We visited him and his wife (my aunt) Masha, a wonderful woman, in Chelyabinsk (§ 5) where they appeared after running away from Vitebsk. (And Yakov was wonderful and jovial.) She was a nurse, worked in a clinic for railway workers and was decorated with the Order of Lenin for long time service there (that was the practice for some time, stimulation of the interest of railway men). Accidentally met people therefore treated her respectively.

I was healed but found partly fit for active service. My speciality was not required and I was demobilized. Anyway, my place would only have been in headquarters, possibly nowhere at all. I had time to see Berlin.

8.2. Inscriptions on the ruined Reichstag, stacks of bricks in the middle part of wide streets, half-starved Germans with backpacks ... *Chlorodont* written on waggons of the underground (called *Untergrundbahn* rather than *U-Bahn* as nowadays) which, for us in the Soviet sector of occupation, did not reach beyond it. As compared with the Moscow underground that advertising seemed almost blasphemous. PKW (Personenkraftwagen) rather than Auto; the toilet in a railway station, *Abort.* In Nazi Germany foreign words were avoided whenever possible and literature was published in the Gothic type. Slogans of a great size in the streets:

Hitlers come and go, but the German nation remains.

That was Stalin's declaration, but missing were the unsuitable words: ... *and the German state* (*remain* rather than *remains*).

I stood once on a tram stop and overheard a remark of a German: *No light* (interruptions) *but the Rathaus* (the district hall, then occupied by the Soviet commandant's office) *burns day and night.* Several times I had to ask some German to show me the way. They answered verbosely, therefore, for me, obscurely. Once, however, a woman answered clearly and briefly, and I looked at her with suspicion. Then it dawned on me: a wife of a Soviet officer! I smiled broadly, saluted her. *Danke schön*! She smiled back. *Bitte schön.* And we parted, content with each other.

Our military knew German badly if at all. A story: a soldier warns the wife of a German farmer in Russian, only the word *der* (instead of the correct *die*) was in German: *Der cow is in the kitchen garden.* I recall Pushkin's story in prose, words spoken in Russian to a Frenchman: *I cannot dormir* (sleep) *in the dark.*

8.3. An announcement in a German newspaper: *Widower, 53, kein P/G* (not a *Parteigenosse*, a non-party man), *totally destitute after bombing, wishes to get acquainted* ... A story from the same source: a postman is confusedly roaming the remnants of the Imperial office; in 1946! he should deliver (an anonymous?) postcard with birthday greetings to Hitler. German formalism!

And how do the Germans cross the road? Many of them wait for the green light even when no approaching cars are even seen. A story: a man continues waiting when the light is green. He does not trust *them.*

Hitler perished in 1945 and his jaws were sent to Moscow for a final identification of the body. A few days they were being kept by military interpreter Elena Rzhevskaya, or, otherwise, by my cousin Lena Kagan. She told me later how she questioned a captured officer of the SS. He was silent and she asked him:

Do you know who I am? – *Certainly! A young and pretty woman.* – *I am Jewish.* And he exploded. – *I will tell everything, only take her away*!

It is persistently rumoured that Hitler had managed to escape to Antarctic, lived there for a long time and died there. If so, he had remained harmless, his whereabouts were hardly known, capture would have been costly and (very important!) previous statements about his death will be embarrassing, so why bother?

8.4. Berlin was separated into four sectors, the Soviet and the three of the Western occupational forces. As an officer, I was allowed to go everywhere, but a patrol arrested two Russian girls who mistakenly came into a Western sector, – after they asked him to show them the way! They turned to me for help, but what could have I done? Told them that I was obliged to assist patrols. An investigation would have followed and possibly their return home if not something worse.

Our military enjoyed the right of free public transportation. A story: a tram conductor in Bucharest demanded payment from two soldiers. Instead, they showed him a Russian inscription left somewhere in the tram: *Odessa. Plant* … A few polite words certainly followed.

In Potsdam a big announcement in Russian on (or near?) a private house: *Jew*. I doubted whether that was a good idea. Father was a careful driver, got his license (regretfully lost) back in 1915, signed by a prince. And still he hired a driver for his *Opel-Kadet*. To find him, he applied to the labour exchange. I doubt whether during all the time of the occupation of Germany there had occurred even one more case of a senior Soviet officer applying to that exchange!

In the artillery school I had practised driving for about half an hour and was afraid of driving. In 1989, before moving to Germany, I got a driving license just in case, but it proved useless: I was still afraid of driving, am psychologically unfit, and, for that matter, people drawing welfare (as I still do) are forbidden to own cars.

8.5. I remember studying theory in a driving school in Moscow. I read *stupitsa* (much, much less known than is its English translation, *hub*). Did not understand, quit reading. Since then I became convinced: here, in Germany, there hardly appeared more than a few understandable instructions on how to use a telephone, a fridge, etc., you name it! Much money is needed for manufacturing such goods, but, when instructions are concerned, businessmen become niggardly. And for good measure you often get an instruction for another model of the bought thing.

But what about the translated instructions? I usually read them in English but am unable to check duly the quality of translation. Incidentally, Dorian assured me that the translations into Arabic of the instructions on Soviet military materials had been incomprehensible (wherefrom that information?), but I thought: how was it with the originals? And in general it is morally difficult to translate properly badly written texts.

9. The geodetic institute

9.1. And so I returned home. Without due thinking entered the Moscow Institute for Engineers of Geodesy, Air Survey and Cartography (Geod. Inst.), formerly the Land Surveying Institute and now a university. Indeed, wasn't I a topographer, even if with the addition of adjective *artillery*?

A fellow student, Yura Rainish, was actually a Jew, but a Ukrainian both by external appearance and name. Was certainly questioned by our valorous *organs* and asked, how he managed to survive for a few years in a concentration camp for prisoners of war.

Just try it out yourself for at least one day.

I recall many knowledgeable and conscientious instructors: A. I. Durnev (what an ugly name of old!), P. S. Zakatov (a future *rector*), B. N. Rabinovich, D. S. Shein (an ancient Russian name), A. A. Izotov (closest assistant of Krasovsky, who is mentioned below), and Professor V. V. Danilov(mentor of my diploma work and womanizer).

I heard that an announcement was placed in our large yard: *Yardman needed, dwelling space* (generally greatly missing) *granted.* Izotov, who had been living precariously, applied.

But how will you be able …? – Yardman in the morning, instructor in the afternoon. – But why …

He explained, got the dwelling place (surely barely habitable), had to remain there for a long time although without being a yardman.

Professor A. S. Chebotarev, chair of *lower* (since later, *engineering*) geodesy, was very influential, a terror for those who defended dissertations. He (1958, p. 579) declared that

For fourteen centuries the Ptolemy system had been holding mankind in spiritual bondage …

Idel'son (1947) published a book which G. V. Bagratuni (future editor of the translation of Gauss' memoirs on the method of least squares) called *algebra* as compared with Chebotarev's *arithmetic*. Yes, he hopelessly lagged behind: did not recognize mathematical statistics, persecuted those who had attempted to introduce its elements in the treatment of observations. He (1951, pp. 8 – 9; 1953, p. 24) even accused Romanovsky (1938) of stating that probability is *described* by the law … Had not Marx declared that philosophers only described the world, although we should change it? Even on the Soviet level this was balderdash.

9.2. The preliminary, so to say, campaign against kowtowing to the West had then already begun, and Romanovsky was one of its victims (but did not seriously suffer). A Resolution of a special conference (*Soveshchanie* 1948) approvingly stated that he *acknowledged his previous ideological mistakes.*

Pearson was a special target of Chebotarev's (and other Soviet statisticians') attacks since Lenin had called him an ideological enemy of materialism. In a posthumous book Pearson (1978, p. 243) as though in turn remarked that

Petersburg [Petrograd] […] *for some inscrutable reason has now been given the name of the man who has practically ruined it.*

Romanovsky had been working in Tashkent University from its establishment in 1918 until death (in 1974). In 1937 he had been dean of the physical-mathematical faculty and in 1938 became deputy of the republican (Uzbek) Supreme Soviet. But in 1929 he (Sheynin 2009, p. 374) wrote to Fisher from Paris (in his bad English):

The GPU [Chief Political Administration], *the most dreadfull and mighfull organization in the present Russia …*

In 1981, V. D. Bolshakov, the rector of the Geod. Inst., Honoured Science Worker (and ignoramus), organized a celebration of the centenary of the birth of that dinosaur. In eight reports (*Izvestia Vuzov, Geodeziya i Aerofotos'emka* No. 6, 1982) Chebotarev was praised to the sky. Bolshakov & Yu. I. Markuze, a clever pocket Jew, pictured him as almost the main follower of Gauss in treating observations.

I had a few times honestly tried to elicit something useful in Chebotarev's *brick* (a Russian expression), in his book (1958), 605 pages long, but each time only became disgusted. And he

(p. 3) *regrettably* remarked that lack of place prevented him from discussing the theory of relativity and quantum theory. Both theories were likely saved from a crushing devastation …

In 1981 the Geod. Inst. properly and worthily celebrated the centenary of the birth of Krasovsky, but Chebotarev? Shouldn't we separate the sheep from the goats (Mathew 25:31)? The latter's jubilee was however needed for glorifying the institute (and its valiant rector).

There was a chair of *military matters* and the second-year students devoted a whole day weekly to military topography but I was freed from that. Then, the *principles of Marxism – Leninism*, lectures by a crippled docent Shneerson. He was head of *Chekvalap* (Extraordinary Commission on the Supply of the Army by Felt Boots and Bast Shoes). The Labour Party won the elections in England, and he told us: nothing will change. Canons and machine guns are needed for that. That's Communist ideology for you.

An instructor in political economy mathematically represented the statement of Marx about commodity-money relations. We, the students, were much better versed in mathematics than he was, and noted some mistake in his rendition. Nevertheless, his attempt was commendable.

BBC began transmitting in Russian and jamming was not yet introduced. Someone declared that he had heard only nonsense, but he did not dare to comment.

I dimly remember my astronomical practical work on the special platform in our yard. It was extremely pleasant to see how the chosen star enters the field of vision of my instrument just at the moment which I had determined beforehand.

9.3. During our senior years we had mostly studied higher geodesy (triangulation, figure of the Earth, etc.). The great Soviet triangulation had been quite reasonably adjusted although without any application of mathematical statistics. Feodosy Nikolaevich Krasovsky, corresponding member of the Academy of Sciences, respectfully nicknamed *Saint Fedos*, was our leading figure. Very ill, he did not lecture anymore but remained chair of higher geodesy. He lived in a house in our great yard, and his colleagues regularly met him there for guidance and consultations. A geodesist by education, for some time he studied mathematics and physics at Moscow University, worked on probation at Pulkova, and in 1916 became professor of the Moscow Land Surveying Institute.

Krasovsky worked out an extremely expedient pattern for the ever widening Soviet triangulation, was a pioneer in the wide application of gravimetric measurements, guided the determination of the best for his time (and still almost the best) figure of the earth (of the *Krasovsky reference-ellipsoid*), educated many eminent geodesists and initially educated another great scientist, Molodensky (gravimetry, geophysics, astronomy).

Practically all Soviet geodesy had been based on the works of Gauss, Bessel and Helmert, and for this science the campaign of 1949 against cosmopolitism was not severe. Later, however, when working on my diploma thesis, I had to obtain special permission for reading foreign geodetic journals. At the time, Father recalled the howls of a pack of monkeys in Kipling's *Jungle Book*:

We are great. We are free. We are wonderful. We are the most wonderful people in all the jungle. We all say so, and so it must be true!

9.4. For some years Krasovsky was the official Soviet representative on the Baltic Geodetic Commission which coordinated geodetic work of the countries encircling Baltic. He became president of that Commission, but in 1938 he was recalled because of his imagined bad health.

Furthermore, the same year the Soviet Union left the Commission under a stupid pretext. As I see it, the real reason was the aim to essentially curtail essentially any ties with the West.

The campaign against cosmopolitism fell into absurdity. *French rolls* became *city rolls*, *English* (= safety) *pins* lost their adjective, *challah* was named *pletyonka* (twist) and it was not Fleming who discovered penicillin. Stalin was preparing for a cold (only cold?) war, raised the poverty-stricken, hungry people white-bled by himself against *external enemies*. He refused aid from the Marshall Plan since it contradicted his criminal plans. Whether the Wise, Dear and Beloved read Béranger or not, he followed the advice of that French poet:

Look out, my friend/When jumping,/Never jump by halves!

Death followed each of his jumps. Here is his alleged statement:

Death of an individual is a tragedy, but death of a million is only statistics!

Actually, the hundreds of thousands of exiled *kulaks* (well-to-do peasants) and alleged *wreckers* were not better than external enemies. It seems that the town population was not seriously bothered by the horrible fate of the kulaks since the peasants greatly benefited during the hungry years (a remark of my brother Leonid).

In 1931 Stalin declared:

We are lagging behind the advanced countries by 50 – 100 years and we ought to run through that distance in ten years (to jump). *Either we achieve this goal or we'll be crushed.*

Read: or we will not crush them. *Oh, coachman! Don't drive the horses* (a folk song). Didn't you ride them almost to death? You are wishing to bring about a world revolution, or, more precisely, to establish a world Stalinate.

9.5. By that time anti-Semitism had fully matured. The Germans had achieved this deed on the occupied territories, and Stalin added his own fuel. The campaign against external enemies inevitably assisted the unprecedented flourish of that obscurantism. Why look for external enemies, when they are right here, among us? That idea was not new at all. The crusaders went on foot across Europe to free the Church of the Holy Sepulchre from the infidels, but en route robbed and killed European Jews, infidels as well!

Stalin likely foresaw and eagerly expected all that to happen: we, Soviet Jews, were least prone to hate the *external enemies*! And here is Mayakovsky (*Azbuka*, Alphabet):

AntiSemits are pleasant to Entente,/Entente is a gang of thugs.

I certainly reject his second line.

Oh, my homeland is a spacious country
Streams and fields and forests full and fair.
I don't know of any other country
Where a man can breath a freer air!

(Translated by A. Basta.) Even a Jew can breath?

The music for most Soviet songs which rather successfully obscured the horrible reality was composed by Jewish composers (Blanter, Pokrass but not Dunaevsky whose son and grandson much later escaped from the Soviet paradise). They often borrowed fragments of melodies from Jewish lullabies and nuptials which they had imbibed with their mothers' milk.

10. Work. The University

10.1. And so, I graduated from the geodetic institute and was sent to work at the Moscow Aerogeodetic Enterprise (no possibilities of post-graduate studies for a Jew). After a while, I became instructor at the Moscow Topographic High School.

We had theodolites of high precision and I organized practical work with them in full compliance with the instruction on primary triangulation. Our gymnasium was on the ground floor and brick pillars at the ends of the gym were somehow fastened to the ground below. Students measured angles between some strokes on the opposite walls and the readings were registered in ink, never by pencil. I am still proud of my work since nothing comparable had been going on in the Geod. Inst. In summer, in my absence, the students measured angles of the city geodetic network. One of them remarked that they had not learned anything new. *How so? The changing external conditions*!

I wished but was unable to continue teaching there, worked in a few establishments and was obliged to carry out elementary field measurements, once on the territory of *state dachas*. One of these dachas was called in common parlance *Kalinin's dacha*. Kalinin was President of the Soviet Union and Stalin's henchman. No one of the people on the very top had been present. My chief came there with me for a preliminary talk with the local administration. My presence was not needed at all, and he later explained: he wished to show me to that administration (= to let them decide whether to allow a Jew to work there).

10.2. This happened during the autumn of 1952, a horrible time. The Jewish *Doctors' plot* was revealed and almost everyone was convinced beforehand that those doctors had destroyed several *leaders of the people*. I had to think twice whether to ask my way; patients coming to clinics refused to go to Jewish doctors. But the main point: it was widely rumoured that all of us, at least in large cities, will be sent to the Jewish Autonomous Oblast in the Far East.

That autonomy was established in 1934 and many Jews had settled there. Gradually, however, Russians became greatly prevalent. And so, I heard many times that Stalin planned to hang publicly those (oh, most certainly guilty!) doctors and then save us from the infuriated crowds by sending us there, where barracks (unsuitable even for sunny Georgia) were already waiting us. Answering some of his henchmen Stalin explained: there is enough room for them since some will perish en route. Indeed, the travel will be murderous and *spontaneous* pogroms will occur.

Some authors doubt those stories since no documents even hinting at those plans had been found. But incomparably more significant is *the complete official silence*! A story: A yardman tells a Jewish tenant that his place in a communal flat was earmarked for NN.

How so? I am living there. – How so? People say that yours is a clever nation!

Brezhnev visited that autonomy and the Jewish head of its administration assured him:

Brezhnev is our brother, but Golda Meir is not our sister.

Brezhnev hardly held any bad feelings against *those* Jews but I recalled the book *My Brother – My Enemy* (Mitchell Wilson, 1952).

The Damned departed and just in time! I was exactly then travelling by train and a conductor, a young girl, was weeping. But the *guilty* doctors were freed (although one of them died in prison) and their *plot* was forgotten.

My late sister-in-law spoke about her relative who was connected with the *organs*. He worked somewhere in the Caucasus, and, together with some others, was obliged to fulfil a monthly quota, to prepare a certain (varying from month to month) number of criminal cases for the courts, among them a definite number of intellectuals and Jews. A planned economy! I myself heard: these numbers had been often surpassed by zealous officials who sometimes found themselves in the same mousetrap.

The father of that sister-in-law was born in Baltimore but a semiliterate registrar wrote *Baltic more* (sea) instead. That greenhorn successfully complained – and was never treated as a true-blue citizen.

10.3. Once I had been working in a dirty Tatar village. There were about twenty of us, mostly students of the Moscow Land Surveying Institute. I was the only calculator and dealt with all the field geodetic work from elementary transits to triangulation of the second order. Many Tatars had purely Russian names; their forefathers were driven into the local river and baptised, all of them at once.

One of us looked after our everyday life (was a business manager of sorts). A former Hero of the Soviet Union and colonel, but I never knew why he was harshly deprived of those title and rank. He told us about his service in the Far East. For many years officers even during their furloughs had been forbidden to travel West further than the Urals. Many of them ruined themselves by drinking, some shot themselves, but the goal was attained: as he stated, the *military preparedness* of the army had been high enough.

During the war an officer from Smersh asked his permission to arrest two soldiers (to be certainly shot by sentence of a court martial). They were mortally guilty! One of them remarked to the other: *Look* (at a photo): *Stalin is in fancy boots, but Lenin wore simple shoes*.

Both soldiers served under the (future?) colonel, so he told the zealous idiot: *Just approach them, and I will shoot you at once*. Then he complained to a familiar higher-ranking officer from Smersh, and that idiot was transferred somewhere. But was he at least reprimanded? And how many military men and civilians had been shot or did long time for suchlike horrible crimes?

Smersh (1942 – 1946), an abbreviation for the Russian *Death to the spies*! was a name chosen by Stalin for an umbrella organization for three independent counter-intelligence services in the army.

Yes, Lenin had been wearing simple shoes but his terrible deeds were obscured by incessant lies. And a question: What shoes had worn other worthy representatives of humanity, from Robespierre to Pol Pot?

The colonel also told us that a military doctor was shot in the presence of an officer formation. Seven times he managed to miss his frontier-bound train.

10.4. I entered the department for external (actually, evening) studies of the mechanical-mathematical faculty of Moscow University. I had not been quite myself, thought of studying mathematics deeper and, as a geodesist in the first place bore in mind the theory of probability.

The first two years of study went by successfully. I translated two books, one from Bulgarian (§ 7.2), the second one, from English (Bomford 1952). It was written on a due level, which was however somewhat lower than attained by our geodesy. Its translation was not easy at all.

And my geodetic diploma was sufficient for teaching in an evening school and even in the Moscow Institute of Food Industry, although only being paid there by the hour. The director of that evening school told a few teachers including me how, during the civil war and being eighteen years old, he went somewhere on a business trip with a wrongly dated document certifying that trip . He was apprehended as a suspicious person, arrested and put into a cellar with dozens of suspected or somehow guilty people. One after another they were taken out and shot. (Petrov denied any alternative.) Then he was called out but he was lucky enough to recall that his name was most usual. *But the first name and patronymic*? He was the wrong Petrov!

In the Food Institute I additionally twice, as it seems, became member of the selection committee. A young girl sat for her mathematical examination but then our director (not yet rector) turned up:

The tangent of 90°? – It doesn't exist. – We do not need such students,
and away he victoriously went.

In those times examiners worked in pairs and we certainly paid no attention to that declaration, but, regrettably, we did not explain the situation to that girl.

10.5. I had to teach some foreign students, Mongolians and Chinese. All the few of the former should have been sent away which is what I said on occasion to the dean of the appropriate faculty. – *Favouritism exists there also* (!). I am sure that my recommendation was too troublesome to be realized.

But the Chinese? *Most praiseworthy* was the general opinion about them. I had two Chinese students and they once asked me how to find out whether a given point was above or below a given plane. A good question, since such problems were not studied then. About two years later I accidentally learned that they both had to transfer to the Moscow Aviation Institute.

Later, in the Plekhanov Institute for National Economy (§ 13) I met students from Africa, not better than the Mongolians. Our native students disliked them since they were much better off. I saw an inscription in ink on a desk:

He was taken off a palm tree and sent to [our] *Institute, USSR*.

While in the former institute, I had also been tutoring, prepared a few Georgians for entrance examinations. They were barely better than the Mongolians.

10.6. My study in the University continued. Principles of Marxism – Leninism: I did not have to be examined once more but it was annoying that the best hours of the Sundays (the days on which lectures for us were read) were given over to that, oh, so important subject rather than to some mathematical discipline.

Political economy (a dated name): for some reason I had to hold the examination anew and only after presenting some written work. One of them was rejected, and I complained to the dean. His assistant read my paper and its review and decided that both were poorly. I do not remember what happened next.

Theory of probability: I did not *feel* it. There were too few lectures, but anyway formulas did not help and the situation only improved after I had begun to study the history of that theory.

The main setback had only occurred after graduation: only then I realized that we were deceived. We had not studied the most important functional analysis. The faculty even decided to call us, in our diplomas, *teacher of secondary school*. That decision was revoked; it seems that one of us had acquaintances with some highly positioned people.

Our department was soon closed; indeed, it was too difficult to become a mathematician by studying on the borderline of the faculty. However, at least some of those who opted for mechanics became able specialists and certainly worked in *post boxes*. One of them noticed me and turned away. It was apparently not comme il faut for an employee of some military establishment to speak with former acquaintances, the less so with a Jew.

Post box was the everyday name of closed institutions whose postal address only consisted of a city (usually a wrong one) and the number of a post box. These numbers had been more or less regularly changed to confuse possible spies but actually confused everyone concerned.

Two of my acquaintances managed to become real mathematicians. One of them worked with Pontriagin, an anti-Semite par excellence, the other is mentioned below.

10.7. After long trying experiences I landed in the Institute for Scientific Information, sector Geodesy of department Astronomy and Geodesy, in the absence of the chief of that department, Professor K. F. Ogorodnikov. He later expressed his displeasure: A Jew! He was not an anti-Semite but afraid of trouble. My knowledge of English (and of more or less German) helped me, and the head of the sector, the late A. V. Kondrashkov, a pluralist who had known me in my student years, ran the risk. He needed an *Englishman* (the translator of Bomford) and I was a mathematician as well.

Ogorodnikov lived and worked in Leningrad and arrived for a few days monthly, apparently not at his own expense. Told us two stories (up to a certain level not criminally persecuted anymore). *The first*: how to draw a one-eyed man? With both eyes? No, too crude. *Draw him in profile from the side of his non-existing eye?* No, that will oppose socialist realism. So *Draw him in profile from the other side. The second*: commentary on a race of an American and a Russian which the former won.

The American ran with all his might but came only next to last. Our guy was in good form and came second.

Ogorodnikov was not sufficiently familiar with our reality. He did not understand why, unlike the Roman Catholic priests those of the Russian Orthodox Church had not participated in the everyday life of their flock. Why? Because that was strictly forbidden.

The *scientific secretary* of our department was L. N. Radlova born in Petrograd and belonging, as I would say, to the old Petrograd cultural milieu. In my scientific work I came across E. L. Radlov, a philosopher and editor of the influential official journal of the Ministry of people's education. And so, I decided to say something pleasant to our Radlova and mentioned him; she was apparently his granddaughter. My good intention backfired:

Yes, he was an idealist, not a materialist, but in those times …

She had been possibly asked about her dubious namesake or grandfather. And she was certainly a relative of another Radlov, a son of E. L. and a producer.

Celestial mechanics was the realm of B. M. Gelfgat, an inveterate mountaineer. He perished somewhere in those mountains, very young of age. In our sector there was V. I. Siniagina, an able and thorough worker. Her brother occupied a high position in the Ministry of agriculture and V. I. retold his story. It was too dangerous to oppose the stupid Khrushchev's *maize campaign* (loss of job will probably follow).

Mister K (as he was named then in foreign newspapers) visited US and thoroughly, as he imagined, studied the American experience. He decided: maize ought to be grown everywhere, up to the region of permafrost. It is difficult to estimate the losses incurred by his imperial stupidity. *We wished for the best, but got the usual*! (A saying invented by a former prime minister, the late Chernomyrdin.)

Yes, Khrushchev wished to show the Americans *Kuzkina mat*, to overcome them in agricultural produce. Some kind of homespun truth was felt in his being, but he was talkative and behaved like *a bull in a china shop* Not only did he bang his shoe in the UN (so that that proverb could have been continued: *or as K in the UN*), he brought the world on the brink of an atomic war (the Caribbean crisis).

10.8. The story of two large-scale speculators in foreign currencies, Rokotov and Faibishenko, is hardly remembered. They bought currencies from the small fry and sold them (to whom?) and certainly fed up the Moscow militia (quite recently *militia* was renamed: *police*). But then Khrushchev found out from a foreign newspaper (apparently was told about it) that such activity was going on in Moscow. He demanded to quench it; he possibly was mainly angered by the bad publicity *abroad.*

Those two had to be arrested, arraigned for their illegal activity and sentenced to do long time. No, that will not do! Too lenient! And Krushchev demanded a change in the penal code. His command was obeyed, the case was heard anew and the perpetrators sentenced to *the highest measure of proletarian humanism* (Voinovich). A blatant violation of a main commandment: *Law is not retroactive*!

The world was outraged, but *our Dear Nikita Sergeevich* (K) *listened* (to the admonishment of the cook) *but continued to gobble up the chicken* (Krylov's fable). And he promised his beloved children: *You will, you will live under communism* (and rashly believed himself in that phantasy).

Fine, children, fine! Only wait a while …

What need do you have for Rokotov?

I'll give you the squirrel/And the whistle as well

(Chukovsky).

A black market was unavoidable and could have been only suppressed by economic measures. A story. Stalin decided to find out the real relative strength of the dollar and the rouble. Three eminent economists had to solve this problem. Those dashing fine fellows exerted themselves and hoisted: 1 dollar = 6 roubles 60 kopecks. Stalin was notified and decreed: 1 dollar = 66 kopecks. Ideology was about ten times more important than economics and the existence of a black currencies market ensured.

That decree was especially harmful for foreign tourists who did not need free education and hardly required free medical aid. Nevertheless, they themselves were not needed, they poisoned our socialist atmosphere. But how about the loss of currencies? Well, do not we have prisoners with their free labour or forests for cutting them down and selling the wood abroad? Wood, rather than timber, why bother?

But what is communism? The naïve Lenin formula (*Soviet power and electrification of all the country*) was forgotten long ago and in 1972 a new definition appeared in the Programme of the Party:

From each according to his abilities, to each according to his needs.

This formula appeared in the 17th century and was borrowed by Marx. A necessary addition was omitted: *Each will get angelic wings.*

10.9. Another employee, A. V. Zenina had been occupied in our sector with photogrammetry. A Russian German, she spoke German fluently but did not write grammatically. She had been previously working in China, then in Comecon (Council for Mutual Economic Assistance [of socialist countries, 1949 – 1991]) which was established as a counterweight to the European Economic Community.

Zenina was delighted by the Chinese meticulousness and their desire to understand everything. Told us that rats were sold in markets and the longer they were, tails included, the greater was their price. A stupid campaign was carried out there: sparrows ate the sown seeds, and they were exterminated (prevented from landing anywhere) by order of Mao Zse-Tung. Insects began to harm much more, and sparrows had to be imported. So much for the wisdom of the Great Helmsman.

Soviet specialists had been living in several rooms in a hotel. The carpet in one of the rooms was decorated with swastikas, venerable Chinese hieroglyphs borrowed by the Nazis. This fact had to be explained to the outraged specialists.

The Czechs at the Comecon invited their Soviet colleagues to their embassy, but no one came. They repeated their invitation in writing, once more in vain. Zenina proudly told that as though they had won a moral victory although actually they behaved barbarously, certainly by order from above: visits to foreign embassies were only allowed for the most *reliable*.

We also had a stylist, L. G. Efanov who had been previously employed by the *Enziklopedia* publishers. They worked under the wings of the High House. Thus, proofs had been printed one after another until no misprints were left. Oh, sorry! That House was the seat of the Central Committee of the Party, of *The Mind, the Honour and the Conscience of Our Epoch*.

Efanov told us that the article *Stalin* could have appeared earlier, but just in case it was decided to publish it in their next volume (certainly with many following articles). Something was wrong in his story (the page numbers in the two volumes did not match it) but anyway the delay from March 1956 to November 1957 led to the appearance of Stalin's portrait occupying a whole page and only moderate criticism in the text. In 1956 the air was much freer!

Efanov also told us about a celebrated photo: Lenin and Stalin placidly sit on a bench. My verse:

Teacher Lenin, Student Stalin,/
On a bench they are a-sitting,/Bloody tortures, wait awhile!/
A respite they did deserve.

They received that photo with a polite request to publish it. The man who was in charge of photos asked, as usual, for the negative. His request was refused under some pretext, he foolishly insisted – and disappeared …

Actually, Lenin sat on that bench alone (but after some alteration my verse is still valid). Many photos are known to have been *doctored*. Those who were later declared enemies of the people were replaced by others, in the first place by Stalin whenever possible and advisable.

Efanov was a singer, but something happened with his spine. He had to quit, but was able to acquire a new speciality. I learned somewhat from him: oblique cases; Roman numerals to be left in Russian texts as they are (XX rather than XXth century); all items of a decision or resolution to be formulated in the same key. Then Efanov noticed that in Russian *vicinity* only existed in the plural form, so that our ε-vicinity was inadmissible! But he kindly agreed to consider that expression as a special professional word. A later spelling dictionary admitted the singular form as well.

Efanov also revealed a secret of the extras, of the artists in the background who have nothing to say. More precisely, they ought to be seen (but not heard) speaking by the audience, so they repeat the same phrase to each other: *What can I say if there is nothing to say*?

10.10. Our neighbours were mathematicians (the journal of abstracts *Mathematics*) and after leaving my job I began to compile abstracts for them. Our institute also had some *closed* departments and I accidentally found out that in one of them a card of foreign scientists was compiled. Those scientists who sympathized with *the first fatherland of the working people* were separated from those who were in captivity of the *rotten bourgeoisie ideology* (the sheep were separated from the goats).

Our institute employed many specialists without scientific titles and therefore poorly paid (I was one of them). I heard that our director asked the President of the Academy of Sciences to allow him to increase their wages. – *I am thinking about your institute least of all.* I am not sure that the actual answer was so rude. But here are stories about the low wages of intellectuals. A megalomaniacal engineer thinks that he is a butcher (meat was only rather easy to buy in a few largest cities). And my relative, a physician in a hospital cried on the shoulders of a few people. He studied for fifteen years (including school), has sound experience, sometimes saves the lives of his patients, but his salary is two or three times smaller than that of people who often were only educated in schools. Without remorse he accepted gifts (usually rather modest).

The job could not have suited me as a mathematician but suddenly (for me) *Biometrika* had published translations of the memoirs of Daniel Bernoulli and Euler on the treatment of observations and I at once delved into the history of the theory of errors. Thus began my scientific work, but my job was nonetheless too dull and some staff reduction seemed inevitable.

11. The seminar on the history of mathematics

11.1. I found a job in the Plekhanov Institute for National Economy (Institute), certainly by using my personal connections, but mostly because a few mathematicians including Kolmogorov had publicly criticized economists. (Even in 1959 L. V. Kantorovich devastatingly criticised them, see § 12.4.) Eminent economists at that Institute became frightened and wished to secure themselves, so I got a position in the laboratory there.

Then I defended my candidate dissertation on the history of the theory of errors, on the borderline between geodesy and mathematics, at the Institute for the History of Science and Technology (Inst. Hist.). In the university, my diploma thesis was on mathematical statistics. It was mentored by L. N. Bolshev, a student of Kolmogorov and future corresponding member of the Academy of Sciences; regrettably, he died early. But still I remained on that borderline especially because of my work in a geodetic journal.

At first, I even thought about defending my dissertation at my alma mater, but decided that I was closer to mathematics. That same Bolshev, now an *official opponent* of my dissertation, had presented a negative testimonial and I took back my thesis.

He worked in the Mathematical Institute, in the department of mathematical statistics, under N. V. Smirnov, and they had been discussing all the theses which their employees received for obtaining testimonials. Bolshev later told me that Smirnov had totally opposed my work, but that he, Bolshev, remarked that it was written on a good geodetic level.

I rewrote my thesis and Bolshev, already the head of the same department since the death of Smirnov, had given a positive testimonial and I defended my dissertation. After some time he asked me whether I had been offended by his first testimonial and I honestly answered: *I myself would have now signed it by both hands*. The second opponent was Maistrov (who died in

1986). I did not then realize that his knowledge of our common subject as well as of foreign languages was slight.

11.2. I heard most favourable opinions about Bolshev and a volume of his collected works appeared after his death. He is mostly remembered in connection with the statistical tables compiled by Smirnov and him. After my defence I came to him several times to hear his advice. He was interested in the history of his science and in addition wished to introduce it into geodesy. In turn, he therefore discussed his thoughts of applying sequential analysis for deciding when it becomes possible to quit observations on a given triangulation station; didn't Gauss act in a similar way? I explained that precision can be more or less reliably estimated only after all the *conditions* (divergences) occurring in a chain of triangles become known; for example, the divergence between the linear dimensions as calculated from the two bases situated at the ends of the chain. And systematic errors are better dealt with when the number of observations is known beforehand. Finally, Gauss never trusted his own estimate of precision since it left out systematic errors, as our instructors at the geodetic institute told us and as I found myself later.

Bolshev's grandfather was a military topographer (= a geodesist), and, strangely enough, the signatures of grandfather and grandson were identical. Bolshev was a member of the editorial board (perhaps its head, even if not officially) of the *Anglo-Russian Dictionary of Mathematical Terms* (1962) which I have been successfully using. He told me that someone suggested to include *Russian roulette* (firing a gun at oneself without knowing whether it was loaded or not) in the word-list of the *Dictionary*. After discovering that meaning Bolshev rejected the proposal; otherwise *we all will be dismissed*. The origin of that term is unknown and it likely appeared in 1937.

11.3. For many years the director of the Mathematical Institute was I. M. Vinogradov, a zoological anti-Semite. His soul-mate was another academician, Shafarevich (who died in 2017 or 2018). His book (2002/2006) is crammed with anti-Semitism, with distortions, is unworthy of any scientist of the lowest rank, of any honest author in general. Here are three examples.

Holocaust is in the same rank with the losses of other nations and its separation *touches my* [his] *moral sentiment* (p. 264). That highly-positioned scum had some sentiments? But of course. Didn't Hitler, the vegetarian, have them? He only wished to oust the Jews (§ 4) and, after his intention failed, he only decided that they must *disappear*.

Then (p. 347), *Sharon visited the Arab sacred object, the al-Haram ash-Sharif* (and therefore defiled it). That object is in Mecca, in a town which the infidels may not enter. Actually, he visited the Temple Mount. Shafarevich apparently thought that no one will check al-Haram, but at least I did. I also note that it is often very difficult to match his statements and the references which was certainly the desired intention. And the third stunning example (pp. 399 – 401) offered by that rascal: *Israel is scientifically empty*!

Two stories about Vinogradov, probably invented. He refused to take on Petrov since *he was half-Jewish*; Ivanov? *His wife is Jewish*; Sidorov? His Russian wife *has a Jewish lover*! The second story: someone from the Caucasus read a worthy report and is quite acceptable for working in the Institute. *He resembles a Jew and it would be unpleasant to see him here*!

Vinogradov allegedly stated that Jews are too talented and can *press back all of us*. Novikov (1995) called Vinogradov an informer (1928 – 1930) and fruitless from the 1930s. Anyway, until 1932 he headed the Demographic Institute but did not even touch demography.

Outstanding statisticians (S. A. Novoselov, V. V. Paevsky) had been working there, but in 1934 the Presidium of the Academy of Sciences closed it since (just imagine!) the attempts to transform its work on a Marxist basis proved unsuccessful (Tipolt 1972, p. 98).

About 1985 Youshkevich publicly remarked that the collaboration with the Mathematical Institute became possible (for Jews like himself).

11.4. I was favourably met at the seminar on the history of mathematics at the mechanical-mathematical faculty of Moscow University. It was guided by a triad: I. G. Bashmakova (ancient Greece, Rome, number theory), K. A. Rybnikov, a true-blue Communist with a photographic memory closely connected with the Moscow Party organs, and certainly A. P. Youshkevich, none of them still alive. Rybnikov was obviously unable to consider me objectively but happily he had not interfered.

Youshkevich was the son of a liberal public figure, of a translator of classical scientific literature (for example, of Leibniz). He probably worked alone, unconnected with any institution, therefore was not persecuted. The son of A. P., a mathematician in his own right and a student of Kolmogorov, is perhaps from 1990 successfully working in the US.

A. P. perfectly well spoke French (although, as he publicly remarked, his language was a bit dated), he knew Latin and German and read English (and envied my pronunciation), mastered the history of mathematics, especially up to the mid-19th century. He enjoyed indisputable international recognition, collaborated with Kolmogorov (see below).

He was ousted from the Bauman Technical School, but found a position in the Inst. Hist. as head of the group on history of mathematics, A group since the powers that be did not wish to see a Jew heading a sector. I translated a few of his manuscripts, visited him at home. Once, in 1969, I came and noticed that he was upset, so what do you think? *An American landed on the Moon, they overcame us*! He was still able to identify himself with those powers!

I commented: *For a long time now I do not apply that pronoun in such cases. – So how then*? *– Overcame the Reds*.

During festive occasions all the typewriters in each establishment were collected in some *safe place* so that no one will be possible to type something *unsuitable*. Once I came to the Inst. Hist. to see Youshkevich just after such an occasion. He was unlocking the door of his tiny room which he occupied with another worker. He saw a typewriter on his table, lifted it up a bit, held it above the floor and let it fall down. *No one ought to put anything on my table*! This happened in the presence of that worker (who came in at the same time). The typewriter did not break.

11.5. I had not invaded the field of any other participant of the seminar; Maistrov was an exception, but he was not influential and Youshkevich was sceptical about him. I got acquainted with one participant, Mikhail Vasilievich Chirikov, whom I had met a few times previously at the evening extension of our faculty. He was a talented mathematician, quite possibly a future doctor of science, but bone tuberculosis overpowered him. He had to quit work as an instructor in one of the Moscow educational institutions. About 1989 he hoped (in vain) to get a computer from abroad and give it away for the general use of historians of mathematics.

Chirikov had been living in a communal flat and was unable to forget how grown up men sobbed and squealed when being dragged out and shoved into Black Maria's (usually inscribed on the outside with the word *Bread*). He needed a special operation only possible abroad. When living in Germany (§ 8), I asked some Mormons to help him. Then I somehow found out that two Mormon Elders (young Mormon preachers serving for two years in some country) visited him in this connection but at the same time began to point him in the only true direction. He did not budge, their visit was fruitless since I did not budge either (neither of us was or became a Mormon), and he died.

11.6. Another participant of the seminar was Kh. O. Ondar from the Tuva Republic in the Far East of present Russia. He lived in Moscow in a student hostel of the University sharing his place with a few students from East Germany (a sure sign of his absolute loyalty). Rybnikov (who else?) took care of him and the mentor of his dissertation was Gnedenko, the ideological leader of probability theory.

Ondar published a few papers on the history of medical statistics in Russia, reported his findings and it became absolutely clear that his mathematics was simply poor. Then he (or Rybnikov?) discovered the correspondence between Markov and Chuprov in an archive in Leningrad, published it (Ondar 1977) and defended his dissertation. Some serious commentaries were certainly written by Gnedenko, the text of the correspondence was essentially corrupted by his ignorance but mostly due to his carelessness and even dishonesty (12 undated postcards from Markov became mysteriously dated).

Ondar died early without achieving anything else, and he is guilty of a disgusting scientific crime of corrupting an important archival source. In 1981 the published correspondence was translated into English complete with most mistakes and some unacceptable modernization of Markov. Later I managed to study that correspondence anew, found a few other letters and discovered dozens of mistakes in the published text but could have only made known the necessary corrections (Sheynin 1990/2011, Chapter 8).

At the time fax machines were not at least generally available, so I am sure that Ondar asked a typist to type the correspondence and barely if at all checked her work.

11.7. I also recall F. A. Medvedev who had been studying the history of set theory (and successfully publishing worthy books) and prematurely died in 1990. I heard his report about Cantor. He stated that churchmen zealously attracted him to Christianity and it sounded as though some gangsters were luring him into their band. An accidental cause prevented me to say that publicly. I read somewhere that Cantor thought of matching Trinity with the existence of a single God. See Koetsier & Bergmans (2005) on the connection of mathematics and the divine.

Medvedev lived for science, was principled and obstinate, he refused to participate in the compilation of *Mathematics of the 19th Century* (*very much ought to be still investigated*). Three or four volumes of that undertaking had been published under the editorship of Kolmogorov and Youshkevich. Gnedenko and I (1978) wrote the chapter *Theory of probability*. In 1992 Birkhäuser translated that volume and I myself translated that chapter.

But first I found out from Youshkevich that that chapter was already being translated by someone abroad, went to the State Protection of Copyright Agency (Agency) and asked the address of the translator. *It is inconvenient to meddle* ... They were simply uninterested, but I insisted, got the address. – *I have already finished*. Youshkevich received the proofs of the previous chapters, sent them without reading to their authors. They slavishly approved the work perhaps with some minor corrections: they had not mastered English and, as I presume, were happy to be known abroad. However, I categorically rejected the translation of our joint chapter. The woman in the US responsible for the work asked A. Shenitzer to check the translations of all the chapters. He was horrified by the work done by a general historian remote from mathematics and all of it was finally rejected whereas Youshkevitch uselessly denied his fault.

About 2000 Shenitzer successively asked Birkhäuser to reprint the translation of that volume, took care of that work and translated anew some part of it. He forgot to notify the Russian co-authors about the future reprint (Russia? Who cares about that mysterious country?). He forgot even me although he knew that I have been living in Berlin. No corrections/additions followed from me and the statement on the title-page of that reprint, *Second Revised Edition,* was still less only partly justified.

Medvedev diligently read foreign literature and copied many sources almost word by word, but was afraid of saying a few phrases in German.

A bit after me there appeared S. S. Demidov and read a report about the axiomatic method. His work earned him an international prize. Youshkevich was well disposed to him and took him on. Bashmakova later remarked that Youshkevitch had thus prepared his replacement. And indeed Demidov became editor of *Istoriko-Matematicheskie Issledovania* (Studies in History of Mathematics) and head of that same group at the Inst. Hist. Quite recently he became President of the International Academy of History of Science; Youshkevich had also been its president.

11.8. In my first report I spoke about Robert Adrain, the American mathematician who derived the normal distribution of observational errors at the same time as Gauss. No one of those present had heard about him and my report was met most favourably although its mathematical part was simply bad. I was too timid and did not criticize Adrain (Sheynin 1965). However, I gradually emboldened and began to call a spade a spade. I (2017a, § 9C) proved that Bessel was an inveterate storyteller as well, that Markov senselessly defended the second justification of the method of least squares since he saw no optimal properties in that method (Sheynin 2006c, p. 81); and that he unreasonably claimed to have transferred probability theory to the realm of pure science (Sheynin 2017a, § 14.1-5); that Gumbel, the active antifascist, became Stalin's henchman (Sheynin 2003b), etc., etc. I summarized all this in a *Black Book* (2017b) with an epigraph from Shakespeare:

There is something rotten in the State of Denmark.

Its later version is due to appear in Poland, in *Silesian Stat. Rev.*

That same Gumbel noted that the *true symbol* of the Soviet Union was not the hammer & sickle, but the bureaucrat's abacus. Had he been a Soviet citizen, for such anathema he would have felt other symbols on his own back. And much later he admitted that in 1926 he was unable to imagine what will become with Russia under Stalin. And here he is a bit later (Gumbel 1927/1991, p. 159):

A hundred million peasants are free from the knout [since Aleksandr II] *and millions of workers may look* [did look but, in 1927, only for a year if at all] *with a great hope on the first attempt at realizing socialism.*

Many Western intellectuals, red (Aragon, Barbusse), and *rosy educated fools* (the *obrazovanshchina*, a word invented by Solzhenitsyn; see also the deeds of the classically educated new generations in § 4.2) had been supporting Stalin in one or another way. In 1922 the naïve Einstein hung a portrait of Barbusse in his study along with a portrait of his own late mother. Feuchtwanger, Berthold Brecht and Willi Bredel were the editors of the Moscow journal *Das Wort* (1936 and later). Not surprisingly several books of the first mentioned were translated into Russian, among them the notorious *Moscow 1937*. This book was based on the author's talks with leading Soviet public and Party figures including Stalin. He even criticized Stalin's cult, but what followed? After some time that book was removed from libraries and several people who read it aloud had been sent to labour camps (as Igor Korneev, my fellow student from the geodetic institute told me).

I also mention Gorky, the humanitarian and the petrel of the Revolution and later its vulture. Many disgusting statements are contained in his booklet (1922). Russian peasants are *apathetic* (p. 9), *very fond of beating no matter whom* (p. 20), special cruelty is in their nature (p. 17). *Like the Jews, who left Egypt were unable to see the promised land the semi-barbarian, stupid and difficult people in Russian villages will die out and a new generation will replace them* (p. 43).

Solzhenitsyn (1974/1989, vol. 2, pt. 3, chapter 2) described him as a supporter of GULAG. Until ca. 1928 many people in Russia believed that they participated in a great mission, but the *Red Wheel* (Solzhenitsyn) continued to roll Russia in all directions and the dying out of the *semi-barbarians* (and people in general) had unimaginably quickened. Gorky himself died in 1936 although possibly not of his grave illness. Rumours about the cause of his death had indeed been heard and in any case his generally known defence of the Jews would have seriously impeded the certainly planned further (§ 9.4) struggle against cosmopolitism.

11.9. The census of 1937 came up with population of 162 *mln* instead of the proudly declared by Stalin himself 170 *mln*. Well, taxes were at once lowered, duration of military service shortened, 2 *mln* people freed from the GULAG ... And you, the credulous intellectual that you are, believed all this? The census was the doing of wreckers (Anonymous 1937, p. 2), the state statistical service decimated, many statisticians found themselves in that same GULAG and few of them were shot. This was Stalin's general rule: scapegoats were invariably found for each of his mistakes. Lincoln's adage,

You can fool some of the people all the time and all of the people some of the time, but you cannot fool all of the people all of the time,

should be continued:

But you can fool almost all of the people for a very long time.

Here is an old proud statement:

Our locomotive, fly forward,/The commune is our station./
No other way do we have,/A rifle is in our hands.

But in 1931 there appeared a down to earth verse:

Torn is my new skirt,/Black is my right eye,/
Scold me not, Mother,/I was not street-wise.

That was my own translation. I even compiled a limerick:

There was an old man in Berlin
As never attempted a grin.
He thought of committing a sin,
Of stealing a bottle of gin
And running away from Berlin.

11.10. In 1990 I published a booklet about Chuprov based on archival sources and translated it into English in 1996 (its second English edition appeared in 2011). He was an eminent *cadet* (member of the constitutional-democratic party which attracted many intellectuals). In the summer of 1917 he went for a few months abroad to study in libraries in neutral Scandinavia, but never returned. Until his death in 1926 he worked intensively and fruitfully. I had unearthed a pamphlet (Chuprov, 1919) whose possibly only extant copy is kept in Paris, in the Bibl. Nat. de France. It lacks a title page and its author is mentioned on p. 16 (on the last page): *A. Tchouprov, professor* [...] in Moscow. That person died in 1908, and the author was certainly his son, *our* Chuprov, possibly afraid of the persecution of his close relatives in Moscow. On p. 4 of the pamphlet we find:

During all his stormy life Lenin strove for power for power's sake without thinking either about Russia or the Russian proletariat. [...] *He was indifferent to the fate of the people.*

Much more is still to come. Chuprov advocated an all-out intervention of the West to crush Bolshevism since the *fabula narratur* [the matter concerns] *the fate of the European culture.*

This is a statement from his letter of Jan. 1919 to someone from the Russian Liberation Committee (30 volumes) kept in the British Library in London. For a century the archivists there had been unable to compile an inventory of those materials (another testimony of the scornful and extremely harmful Western attitude to Russian science and culture). The quotation above is from Add 54437, pp. 123 – 128, the only code known to me.

12. Economics and statistics

12.1. In the laboratory I got acquainted with Irina Kantor. Her father did time, and it really served him right! He was a member of a group of highly positioned Jews in the Moscow Automobile Plant named after Stalin the Damned. They planned (can you imagine!) to dig a tunnel under the Moskva River and blow up the Kremlin.

I also found out the deceit (partly caused by ignorance) in economics. First, the so-called matrix methods for compiling economic plans for separate enterprises. A matrix is a rectangular or square (in economics, numerical) table. Mathematicians add them up, multiply and perform more complicated operations on them. But the economists? They simply wrote *matrix* instead of *table*, became more respectable and never refused to cash in on that novelty. And in general, as soon as money becomes available, charlatans appear as though spontaneously generated.

Second, correlation analysis which was greatly facilitated with the advent of computers. Some economists began to investigate the manufacturing of commodities at separate factories/plants by means of that analysis. Here is a prime later example, the doctor thesis of Petrov, director of a similar laboratory of the Institute, see also

§ 13.11. I saw the published abstract of that thesis, and this is what I discovered.

The initial data hardly belonged to a single statistical population and the number of their items was about twice less than that of the investigated economic indications; the choice of those indications was not explained and their possible interdependence was passed over in silence; the formulas applied were anonymous and the conditions of their validity not mentioned; the correlation table of the dependence between the indicators was quite unnecessarily calculated to five significant figures, most of the items were near to 1/2, i. e., barely helpful, and no use of that table was mentioned.

The Scientific Council of the Institute did not include any mathematicians and its only statistician was ignorant of mathematical methods. It approved that rubbish and it was also approved by the Supreme Attestation Committee. The Council should have refused to consider a (pseudo) mathematically oriented work and, anyway, its members should have abstained from voting definitely.

A few years later Petrov was exposed as a plagiarist (his Abstract was compiled from about twenty sources!). Still later he was found guilty of bribe-taking and sentenced to long imprisonment on probation! I think that such long sentences were never softened in the former Soviet Union.

12.2. Introduction of mathematics into economics (which happened abroad long ago) should have begun with Marx but this was impossible. About 1970 there appeared a jubilee edition of the Russian translation of *Das Kapital*. Splendid bibliographic information without a single comment of any other kind! The same happened with Engels' *Dialektik der Natur*. He properly stated that almost every substance was known in all three states, and so it remained although the *almost* became wrong.

Mathematical ignorance of the Institute's staff was not rare at all. A professor of philosophy calmly stated that he was not familiar with integrals and a docent of the chair of finances (!) proudly announced to me that she had happily forgotten mathematics long ago. So what exactly did she forget? The criterion of divisibility by 3.

Some attempts at the introduction of mathematics had been made in Novosibirsk, but here they were rejected lock, stock and barrel. Previous work in that direction (Bortkiewicz in 1906 – 1907, in German) was hardly known.

The top economists did not tolerate any quantitative theories and kept the Marxist doctrine in its primordial state by a cherished principle:

Quality ought to be taken into account in accordance with the essence of the matter.

The *essence*, however, was simple:

Drive off the mathematicians from our own watering hole, swim in the indicated direction! A qualitative theory will allow it. And

Statistics should reveal and quantify the Marxist laws and regulations.

Cf. Süssmilch's main idea: statistics ought to reveal the divine laws of population.

But Buniakovsky (1866, p. 154), the vice-president of the Imperial Academy of Sciences, declared:

Whoever does not examine the meaning of the numbers with which he performs some calculations is not a mathematician.

I overheard a conversation of two members of the chair of political economy about the announced heightening of prices of furniture, crystal wares, cars and some other commodities. In about five minutes they had discussed this topic, justified that measure and calmed down. I felt that they were prepared to justify everything, but they had not even thought why the heightening was necessary or why and by how much was it different for different items.

12.3. Statisticians had been probably afraid of working together with mathematicians. I recall a statement by the late Pope Johann Paul II:

The attempt to prove the existence of God is tantamount to lowering Him to the level of living creatures.

Almost suffice it to replace God by the Marxist doctrine. Isn't communism a religion of sorts?

Once I had to go to the Central Statistical Directorate (CSD): a leading economist needed to find out how many specialists of some kind did we have. So I spoke to an employee there.

Sampling was hardly known to them. He opened a great sheet of data and I saw many pencilled figures with traces of an eraser. In *higher* geodesy such registration was absolutely inadmissible and anyone guilty would have been kicked out. He showed me a figure, then erased it, found somewhere another figure and entered it instead.

And what about the all-powerful Gosplan (State Planning Commission)? Deficit in usual goods, pushers from enterprises who had to get raw materials and components *scheduled by Gosplan* from cooperating plants and to glean *cuff information* (data written on cuffs in a restaurant during talks with responsible workers of other plants).

Such were the everyday difficulties in practical economics. The problems which faced Gosplan were infeasible the more so because of the fluctuations in foreign currencies and since political decisions cancelled any economic plans (cf. Stalin's volitional decision in § 10.8).

And here is an example of quite another kind. Alaska became a state and the national flag had to be altered. And so it was, but only a year later, otherwise the only enterprise which produced these flags would have gone broke. An economist from the Institute told me that he was able to prove that Gosplan is (could have been?) working properly, but I proposed him an easier problem: invent a perpetual motion machine. The Party dealt with the unavoidable economic discrepancies by robbing Peter to pay Paul: provide certain raw materials to plant A by withdrawing them from plants B, C, …

12.4. Some more about Soviet statistics. In 1954 a conference on that science organized by the Ministry of Higher Education, the CSD and the Academy of Sciences was held in Moscow (Anonymous 1954). Strange statements were heard there!

Only the revolutionary Marxist theory is the basis for developing statistics as a social science (p. 41).

Statistics does not study mass random phenomena which anyway do not display any regularities (pp. 61 and 74). And here is Ostrovitianov (p. 82), the vice-president of the (not Imperial anymore) Academy of Sciences:

Lenin had completely subordinated the statistical method of research […] *to the class analysis of the rural population.* It is impossible to maintain that *the same methods of research are applied* in stellar astronomy and economics.

Lenin *adapted* …and never claimed to have *subordinated* statistics.

You do not understand anything except Marxism? Then keep silent, people will decide that you are clever … At that same conference Kolmogorov (p. 47) had indirectly stated the opposite. He also accused foreign statisticians in that they did not understand the essence of some studied matter and reasonably said nothing about Soviet statisticians. Anonymous (1955, pp. 156 – 158) is another source from which it follows that Kolmogorov had not mentioned population statistics, a touchy subject: too many had perished in GULAG!

But perhaps the year 1954 is too remote? Here then is Kantorovich (1959, p. 60), the future Nobel prise winner:

As the latest discovery in the field of economics we are offered, for example, the propositions that the law of value does not govern but only influences and that the means of production are not simple commodities but commodities of a special kind.

Evasions instead of formulas! The criticism was clearly directed against the ostrovitianovs who did not allow even to think about mathematics in economics.

12.5. In 1960 another conference was held (Voprosy 1961). Kolmogorov (Birman 1960, p. 44) stated there that it was necessary to move to a new stage in political economy and that

The main but difficult aim is to express the desired optimal state of affairs in the national economy by a single indicator.

Read: ... *independently from the law of value.*

But do we need Kantorovich, and why should we listen to Kolmogorov? We haven't been born yesterday! Here is Maria Smit (1961, p. 294), corresponding member of the Academy:

Utterly feeble are the adepts [why not *stooges*?] *of the bourgeoisie political economy in the face of the reality horrible for them. Contrary to them, the power and vitality of the economic doctrines of Marx and Lenin consist entirely in ...*

Just behold! Where did she discover Lenin's economic doctrine? And why did the *power and vitality* ... disappear? That same Smit (1930/1931, p. 4) lustfully noted (literal translation):

The crowds of arrested saboteurs are full of statisticians.

She herself probably informed on the *enemies of the people* still at large and her grammatical merit is outstanding. And (Smit 1934, ignorantly): Gaus (her spelling) and Pearson are guilty of subduing reality to formulas. This troglodyte was editor of the statistical part of the first five or six volumes of the first edition of the *Great Sov. Enc.* (who else?). It is impossible to discover what crimes she had perpetrated there against science.

During my work in the laboratory, Kosygin, the prime minister, carried out an economic reform. Some indicators were changed (*sold*, in the Soviet sense, i. e., taken by other enterprises, instead of *manufactured* production), engineers and technicians received bonuses for successful work. I cannot say anything about the results thus achieved, but one point is certain: something should have been (and actually was?) given to ordinary working people.

13. The chair of mathematics. The Institute in turmoil

13.1. I soon transferred to the chair of mathematics as a senior instructor, then as an acting docent, but continued to study intensively the history of probability and statistics. A new chair appeared, V. I. Ermakov, from a *post box* concerned with space flights. An honest man whom the *box* weaned off from classics. He even took down the hung portraits of our geniuses (apparently a set of portraits was long ago distributed to various educational institutions). Among them I recall Gauss and Chebyshev and certainly Newton. This action jarred on me and I submitted a request: Sell me the *unneeded portraits of classics of all times and nations.* The portraits reappeared but Ermakov did not change his attitude towards me.

The atmosphere however worsened. Ermakov began to take on ever more instructors and docents (and even a professor) from his *box*, politically blind (which was felt) and wholly oriented towards applied mathematics. I recall Taras Shevchenko (I forgot his patronymic). Once I asked him which language is more usual for him, Ukrainian or Russian, and he was unable to decide. By his nature he was a Feldwebel (German sergeant major of old) with a thunderous voice and an inveterate executor of any Party command. Many years later, when jobless, I suddenly noticed him from a window of a trolleybus. He stood confusedly and simply clad on a street in the centre of Moscow. Could it be that such a Feldwebel was discharged?

13.2. Other members of the chair still remained. There was Grigory Lvovich Ginsburg, a mediocre mathematician but a honest and politically blind man, a former navigator in long-haul bombardment aviation with 99 operational flights, a major retired with full-dress uniform (with the right to wear it with shoulder-straps).

But why not 100? Because 100 merited a Hero of the Soviet Union. I happened to hear an interview of a Soviet general transmitted from Israel.

Are there really more Jewish Heroes than Russian? – No, that would have been impossible. But relatively, yes (even without Ginsburg).

Previously he had also been teaching at a military aviation school, and proposed a question for his cadets.

You must destroy a target in Washington. You approach it, but suddenly see an American fighter. Your action?

One of them: – *I attack*. And you? You? Both will attack.

No, you haven't understood anything. You have a military goal, you have flown many thousand miles, yours is a bomber with crew rather than some fighter – and you wish to risk!

But what should we do? – What, indeed! Shout <u>*Mother country*</u>! *And dive into the nearest cloud.*

Washington testified about Stalin's crazy plans (and Ginsburg's false patriotism). Here are the words of S. P. Korolev, the main Soviet rocketeer (and former inmate of GULAG), see Tikhomirov (2007, p. 145):

Almost each week Stalin had been asking me, when our rockets will be able to reach Washington.

The cadets did not betray Ginsburg, otherwise it would be probably stated: *Ideologically unfit to be an instructor* (Mother country!).

Ginsburg lost his health and died about 1982.

13.3. I strained my voice, inhalations proved useless but I managed to continue somehow my work until the end of the academic year. In the summer, I went to Professor Aleksandrov, one of the two most eminent otolaryngologists. He consulted privately which was an extremely rare event. A real landlord he was! He did not *speak*, he laid down his opinion without bothering to check whether his patients understood him. He told me that nothing could be done. A bit later I came to know that a financial inspector had pestered him and that he quit consulting privately. Perhaps he was thus compelled if some patients had complained.

Father secured me an appointment to the second most eminent specialist, Professor Zagorianskaya who only consulted singers from the Bolshoi. She had a look at my vocal chords and advised me to go to Strelnikova, a semi-official practitioner of breathing gymnastics. I healed myself after three visits! So much for the official otolaryngologists. Strelnikova told me that songs ought to be sung by the diaphragm rather than throat which was the secret of bel canto. Another story from her: a famous singer (whose name I forgot) from the Kiev Opera continued to sing during the German occupation of the city. Collaborator! He was sent to a labour camp but survived and even resumed singing. Perhaps he sang in the camp for the turnkeys.

13.4. I read lectures on the differential and integral calculus on the usual dated level for students of the faculty of commodity research in foodstuffs and felt that my work was almost useless. I thought, and still think, that students of such specialities need a special course in elementary mathematics plus general information about that calculus.

I also had to examine external students by asking them to explain their own written tests often compiled by other people or copied from others. For them, explanation was difficult!

A new attitude was introduced. More socially acceptable students (those who had previously worked somewhere, even for a short time) had been indulged and their knowledge certainly suffered. In 1921 fifteen professors of the Petrograd University headed by Markov unsuccessfully protested against similar measures (Grodzensky 1987, p. 137).

I compiled an educational aid which followed my lectures and it was put out in our printing-house. I tried to explain the text in the best possible way. For example, I provided a bit more information than it was necessary: uniqueness of the *particular* solutions (of a differential equation).

One of my students was very thorough but mistakenly wished to learn sufficiently from a *single* source. She should have perhaps become a bibliographer. Once during classes I told her: *You know all this. Better find out how are the prime numbers distributed.* She started to write something, then I stopped her, but at least I told her something.

I also read a short course on linear programming and also felt myself unpleasantly: practical application of that section of mathematics was too difficult and, furthermore, the students were sure to forget almost everything because of their insufficient general education. Such a course should have been practically supported.

13.5. And then came a new rector, B. M. Mochalov, *The Bubble*. He was obviously commanded to oust as many Jews as possible and in any case gladly began to implement this most important goal. For good measure he also ousted many honest employees and took on newly fledged and half-educated doctors of science in their stead. He thus raised the official standing of our Institute.

N. K. Druzhinin, chair of statistics, left us, apparently of his own volition. An honest man, unversed in mathematics; he was the president of the Scientific Council which approved the doctor dissertation of Petrov (§ 12.1). A self-confident and impudent ignoramus, but a doctor of science, appeared in his stead. Once I came to Druzhinin's place. His wife was Jewish and we drank tee with matzo. *I oppose anti-Semitism.* Among his books I especially liked *Khrestomatia* (1963). He told me that at some international conference he had convinced American participants that the relative impoverishment of the working people (indicated by Marx) was real. But did he think about the situation of the working people at home?

13.6. The total duping of the entire population which went on for several decades was effective, cf. the Linkoln's adage in § 11.9 and Ogorodnikov's mistake in § 10.7. My relative, an intrusive but narrow minded person, unconditionally agreed with some high-positioned administrator: Sakharov, who was exiled, harassed all the time and isolated from the outer world, did not deign to come even to the yearly conference of the Academy of Sciences!

And one of my students agreed with his uncle, a minister:

We are giving <u>them</u> everything, but <u>they</u> …

Oh, certainly! But only after further increasing an unnecessary military might, developing the national economy (mostly in the military direction) and satisfying the ever increasing and justified demands of the hard-working elite! In practice, almost according to Marx, the population got as much as was needed for life and its modest expansion. So ministers were also duped …

Our National Emblem is clear to all:
Hammer and sickle are side by side.
Forge or cut, cut or forge,!/What you get is blood from stone.

Take a major of the KGB who had been dealing with some apparatuses. He grew up in the same communal apartment with my future wife, and their relations were always cordial. He was honest and politically blind. The invasion of Afghanistan was allegedly necessary to prevent the Americans to do the same, but I told him that they had neither political (after Vietnam) nor military possibility for that. – *That comes from the enemies' voices* [from BBC etc.]. A high ranking officer from the mightiest agency, also duped!

The invasion was necessary (even contrary to the warning of the General Staff) for continuing WWIII (West Berlin, Korea, Vietnam, Africa) and applying the hoarded and morally aging armament and, anyway, a short victorious war was good for the morale of the population. All happened the wrong way round and, what was incomparably worse, it awakened the militant tendencies of Islam.

The command for the invasion was signed by Brezhnev, but I suspect that the real motive power (in Russian: the *grey cardinal*) behind the Kremlin throne was Suslov, the chief ideologist.

13.7. And then, especially during the last years of the Soviet Union, life went from bad to worse. I heard a remark of an apparently badly educated and perplexed woman:

We are working all the time, our situation should have been improving, but somehow this is not happening.

Sancta simplicitas! As though something depended on ordinary people. For a long time educational institutions had been especially attentive to their external departments. This opened the doors to working people but lowered the level of education. And there were too many institutions but not enough schools preparing technicians. At least one cause of this bad situation was ideological: the desire to show the damned capitalists how many engineers, agronomists etc. are graduating here, in our great country!

About 1990 an engineer who had regularly participated in the attestation of welders, those extremely responsible workers, told me: previously, if the examined hadn't known something important, he did not pass. Nowadays, however, we tell such candidates the answer to our question.

Visits to physicians of many specialities became much more difficult. In 1975 Father was admitted to the famous Botkin hospital in Moscow. An after-operational complication occurred: a suppurative inflammation (and he died soon afterwards). But even in the mid-19th century Florence Nightingale insisted that the relative number of such complications was the real indication of the work of a surgical hospital or ward.

Once a doctor came to his room occupied by six patients, announced something and went away. Father's hearing was bad and he hadn't even attempted to understand her. Again F. N.: she registered many similar incidents although concerning nurses; apparently, she had not even thought about doctors. Another incident: the doctors' round began half an hour later than usual: they held a conference, obviously discussed something important. Certainly, they heard political information!

I myself became a patient of the equally famous Sklifosovsky clinic. The premises of my ward were insufficient, other conditions also poorly and the toilets were disease-breeders. I recalled a naïve question of a foreign tourist:

Why don't you have toilet paper in your public toilets?

Because toilet paper was difficult to come by and would have immediately disappeared from the toilets, and because no one from above thought about such luxuries (actually, about some necessary medical supplies).

13.8. From about 1985 the infant mortality began increasing and was explained away by improved statistics concerning Central Asia. This was not really convincing and troublesome since that indication was very important.

Sausage trains began coming to Moscow, regional trains covering two or three hundred kilometres and crammed with passengers from places suffering from acute deficit of foodstuffs. They bought up as much meat and sausages as possible. Those goods were sold in restricted quantities, but the shop assistants sold them much more though overcharged them and gave them shortened weight much more impudently then usual.

13.9. Again our Institute. Mochalov had another occupation. He invited young female instructors to his study and undressed them. His beloved practice became known, but the victims steadfastly denied everything.

I found out accidentally about the existence of a closed sociological sector apparently manned by former employees of the *organs* free from any statistical knowledge. They compiled a questionnaire which was printed in many copies and sent to all the chairs. Each of us was *orally* ordered to answer it. One of the (quite unacceptable) questions: *Will you intercede for an assaulted man in the street*? True, there were no questions about venereal diseases. Professor L. B. Novak (from the *box*) completed the questionnaire aloud and laughingly said: *Yes, I will.* I refused to answer it. For one thing, answers must have been voluntary and Ermakov wisely did not say a word.

Bribery flourished. L. E. Ulitsky, a late professor of the Institute, told me that a friend had shown him a notebook with a list of (Moscow?) institutes and the money necessary to secure entrance to each. He was present in Mochalov's study when the rector received a call from the (first?) Party *secretary* of the Crimea. He asked Mochalov to *mind* his daughter who will apply for admittance and Mochalov proudly told those present about this request.

And I thought: How much and whom did Mochalov himself pay for becoming rector? His own scientific work, as I heard, wasn't worth a tuppence. Much later I heard from a reliable source that the incomparable Gorby, while still the main Party functionary in Stavropol was nicknamed *The envelope*: he regularly received money (in envelopes) from underground businessmen.

13.10. I knew a young man, Vladimir Vlasov. He served somewhere at the frontier, was therefore considered quite reliable and invited to enter some militia educational institution. Graduated as lieutenant of the militia, began working and immediately quit. That was against bylaws and a scandal erupted. He insisted and took off his uniform. He obviously refused to participate in some dirty doings and became a bus driver. I asked him whether his job was serene. *Oh, certainly*!

But here is the main point. My son became acquainted with some high-ranking militia administrator, told him about Vlasov: *If you need an honest man* … The administrator wrote down Vlasov's address, but never called him. Honest people were only needed for servicing the high and mighty.

And here is Novikov (1995, p. 58) once more:

Anti-Semitism became the Party's general line after stealing [embezzling state money] *and corruption.*

So how needful were Mochalov and Petrov! As to stealing and corruption, the previous motto *Pillage the pillaged*! was transformed: *Pillage whatever you can*! In Berlin, there is a Russian House (as it is usually called), a great and imposing building in the centre of the city. And suddenly it was discovered that it unlawfully belonged to a private German firm. A German court returned the Russian House to the Russian state! And where is the money accumulated by the Party? Dissolved like mist.

Members of our chair participated in the entrance examinations. I was never invited (certainly not!) and did not invite myself (once more: certainly not). We found out that at least one of us who examined the entrants received a list of those of them whom he had to evaluate quite positively and was permitted to add one more name to that list. That practice could have existed for many years and was conducive to the multiplication of useless specialists.

13.11. About 1972 I was talked into pluralizing at the laboratory for assisting the study of some subject connected with mathematical methods in economics. Petrov, the chief of the laboratory, was a swindler par excellence. Some of my friends found out that he had copied his candidate dissertation from two student diploma theses. They were afraid of divulging their finding but I only later understood the real reason of their silence, see below. As soon as they informed me, I passed that information to the chair whose place Petrov was sure to occupy after becoming doctor of science. Too late! The period of storing diploma theses ended, and the testimony was destroyed.

Petrov zealously ousted Jews from his laboratory and probably fed up Mochalov at its expense. He was therefore allowed (no other expression seems possible) to defend his doctor dissertation (see § 12.1). One of my students asked permission to miss some classes: she intended to come to his defence and present him flowers. I agreed but unwisely added: *But what if he fails? His thesis is rather feeble*. Oh, my! She was Petrov's niece, and my job at the Institute had to end although I defended myself for a long time.

My friends discovered plagiarism in the published abstract of Petrov's dissertation, began to inform various Party and educational organizations about it and one of them was severely reprimanded for slandering an honest scientist! Then, however, academician A. G. Aganbegyan from the troubleshooting Novosibirsk caused a fry. On Oct. 28, 1979, an appropriate article appeared in the newspaper *Sozialisticheskaya Industriya,* Petrov's doctor diploma was annulled and the Institute's Scientific Council deprived of the right to discuss doctor dissertations. Petrov was also punished for subsequent doings (§ 12.1) and died, perhaps in 2010. Mochalov also died but had time to read the article *The lessons of the Mochalovshchina* [of the Mochalov phenomenon] in the newspaper *Moskovsaya Pravda*. I ought to add that I had not seen any of those two newspaper publications about which one of our economists told me.

I return to the beginning of the Mochalovshchina. Almost a hundred anonymous letters had been sent to various organizations about the situation in the Institute. Special texts had to be written on each of the Institute's typewriters to help to detect the authors of the anonymous letters. Someone calling himself Mochalov had subscribed to the journal *Pig-Breeding* and

Mochalov made a fool of himself by exposing that *mistake*. Note: each Party member had to subscribe to a Party newspaper and a Party journal. A pretty penny for the Party!

Various commissions came to investigate the situation in our Institute (which was clear to anyone willing to amend it). Bolshakov, who became rector of the Geod. Inst. (§ 9.2), headed one of them. He likely was a good friend of Mochalov and an ignoramus. Bolshev told me that Bolshakov became doctor of science in spite of Kolmogorov's harshly negative opinion written for the Supreme Attestation Committee. (I suspect that Bolshev compiled a draft of that document.) Some powers needed a *proper* rector! I heard that Bolshakov was connected with the *organs* and became a stern rector, another Mochalov, although in his student years he had been quiet as a mouse. He did not however need to oust the Jews: not many of them (of us) had been in geodesy.

At first, the majority at the Institute's Party committee had been opposed to Mochalov, but its struggle was rather feeble: each was justifiably concerned for his own skin. One of the main oppositionists was the extremely cautious L. I. Abalkin, chair of political economy and *secretary* of that committee, an orthodox Marxist who became an academician (and an adherent of the free market!). In those times he had been repeatedly taken away somewhere and compiled reports for Kosygin, the prime minister.

Later the Party committee declared that working together with Mochalov was impossible but the higher Party organs were apparently happy to hear it. The committee was elected anew and Mochalov won. He sacked one of his main opponents, Pakhomov, a clever Yakut by birth and Russian by name, adopted by Rákosi, the Stalinist leader of Hungary who had to emigrate and live in Moscow. Pakhomov went to court. Just then Rákosi died and someone had to accompany his dead body back to Hungary and Pakhomov was the proper man for that. *No, I cannot go; my case will be heard at court.* Oh, nonsense, everything was possible for the Party and Pakhomov was immediately reinstated (but finally ousted).

I came to know later that Pakhomov was connected with the *organs*, so that most opposition to Mochalov was monitored from above. This explained why Petrov's initial plagiarism was not revealed. Pakhomov's followers had been puppets in his and Party's hands. Mochalov and Petrov were dearly needed!

14. My scientific work. The Lenin library

14.1. My scientific work proved successful but I had to learn French (§ 2.4). From the very beginning I decided to publish my contributions abroad (it was then more or less possible). There were (and still are) too few outlets for history of mathematics and I was afraid of becoming a hostage to the regime. First, the doors abroad could have been barred (which practically happened) and I had to hurry; second, such manner of publication could have been considered barely permissible for me: the work of really objectionable scientists became unavailable; it just ceased to exist.

My strong sides were the knowledge of English and a tendency, strengthened by a wide education, to comprehensive descriptions. One historian of mathematics (Eugene Seneta) even complained to me: after my publication the appropriate theme is closed! (See for example my later discussion of the alleged law of small numbers, 2008a.) I should have answered properly, but still was too timid.

Extremely important was the possibility of working in the *Leninka* (Lenin, now Russian State Library). Lacking literature was for free ordered from other libraries at home or abroad. The Library was so rich that the literature published in the 18th century was ordered in the usual way. Here, in Germany, the rules are much stricter: such literature is valuable!

Many knowledgeable employees had been working conscientiously but earned crumbs. Here, many librarians are amazingly ignorant, barely care about their duties (or even do not understand them properly) and, at least until recently, had been earning a worthy salary. The international *do not care a damn* is much more proper for the life outside former Russia.

Leninka had a newspaper hall, a hall for new books and bulletins on new acquisitions were published but nothing similar is in the Berlin State library (a newspaper hall is in another Berlin library).

However, as a rule only people with scientific titles were allowed to enter and professors and doctors had a special hall. In 1990, after becoming a corresponding member of the International Academy of History of Science, I was admitted to that hall. Comfort, serenity, books are even allowed to be taken home. Here, absolute democracy: school students and professors are admitted and treated alike. Copying is allowed; in Moscow, copying was extremely difficult since the facilities were inadequate (easy only for professors), and only done by a special worker; copying of general literature (say, of Tolstoy) was not allowed since Solzhenitsyn, for example, was taboo. I had to persuade that worker that the law of large numbers had no connection with ideology.

In Moscow, a militiaman stood at the entrance, a holster (empty or not?) at his side, and had a good look at the visitors going home; here, only a semblance of check. Books disappeared both there and here. There, partly because copying was difficult; here, many Russian books disappeared and probably surfaced in libraries of the newly independent states of the former Soviet Union.

In Moscow, I sometimes read books with invalidated stamps of German libraries (*Kriegsverlust*, war loss). G. K. Mikhailov, an eminent historian of mechanics, told me that he had bought a book with a German stamp in a second-hand bookshop in Moscow and presented it to its former owner, the Berlin Staatsbibliothek. Its director was pleased, promised to put that book on show. And so, some of the books taken in lieu of reparations landed in private hands.

14.2. The powers that be had not appreciated *Leninka* although a similar treasury only existed in one more place, in the Library of Congress. *Leninka* was subordinated not to the Supreme Soviet, not even to the Council of Ministers but to the Ministry of Culture and all the readily gradually declined with the Soviet Union. Its new director, an obvious time-server, allowed to construct a line of the Underground under the book depository. It became dangerous for entering. I do not know what became later.

A necessary second depository was opened in a suburb of Moscow and the librarians sometimes did not know where to direct our orders for literature.

Much literature landed in the special depository, was only available with special permission, and never recovered. One of the volumes of Mendeleev's works contained his papers about gun powder, and that volume had been kept in the special depository in spite of its hopelessly dated contents. And only that volume of his works is lacking in the Berlin Staatsbibliothek.

14.3. Literature ordered by readers from other libraries and temporarily obtained by the *Leninka* was shamelessly microfilmed. Once I noticed a file of the London *Times* on a counter in the newspaper hall. A librarian held it under her elbow, did not tear herself from looking at the far end of the hall and ignored my naïve request, *May I* … Then there appeared a man somehow resembling a foreigner accompanied by an ordinarily looking woman. They walked along the hall and went out … and the file of the *Times* promptly disappeared. That was an example of duping foreigners.

Another restriction concerned religion (certainly *non gratis* in those times). I ordered the Russian translation of 1899 of Pascal's *Pénsees* and certainly did not mention its subtitle: *Thoughts about religion.* The book came to the librarian of my (not yet professorial) hall which meant: decide whether to allow its reading or not. I was known as an omnivorous reader and got the book at once.

In Moscow, only one English newspaper was available (in a restricted number of copies), the organ of the British Communist Party, *Daily Worker* (later named *Morning Star*). I managed to buy it rather often to improve my English. For me, a foreigner, its language seemed quite good and some of the materials were interesting. I remember a verse

Overworked and underpaid, that's the London Fire Brigade

and a foolish remark: representatives of two enterprises do not themselves pay for a business dinner, so why Tom, Dick and Harry from the same enterprises have to pay for a dinner together? And a remark by the Editor of the Woman's Corner: *My monthlies stopped to the delight of my husband.* Suchlike frankness was unheard of in the Soviet Union. Finally, a letter likely from an industrial worker who asked another working man whether he considered himself a proletarian.

Certainly not, I have a profession. – His profession? A dustman.

If I remember correctly, this letter had to do with a discussion about the relevance of the term *proletarian*.

I had been giving my manuscripts to Youshkevich who was a subeditor of Truesdell's *Arch. Hist. Ex. Sci.* (*Archive*). He approved them (later I understood: he was too lenient) and sent them for publication. Truesdell was a most eminent scholar, a mechanician in the first place and an earnest historian of exact sciences. He mastered the main European languages (probably including Italian), *spoke* Latin and perfectly well knew his own native tongue. He wrote me once that he felt himself as though sitting in the last trench and defending English against the slipshod lingua (as I would say) of foreigners. He required a clear style, certainly did not like passive sentences, hardly tolerated newspaper clichés. He replaced my *achieved pecuniary benefit* by *made a lot of money* and my somewhat dated *waste paper basket* by *bin* (not even by *waste bin*). Once, in a letter to him I even wrote *sure* with an h!

At first I had been disgusted by his *fault-finding*, then understood my mistake, began to write more carefully (also in Russian!) and am extremely grateful for his efforts. Russian authors do not set high store by style.

About 1987 I met Truesdell at an international conference in Moscow and asked him to explain a curious event. He published a paper by Grattan-Guinness which meant that it was communicated by a subeditor, but in the next issue of his *Archive* another subeditor (H. Freudenthal) mercilessly criticized it. How was that possible? Truesdell explained: he disliked (but had to publish) that contribution and asked Grattan-Guiness to withdraw it. Instead, the latter declared that he, Truesdell, was hopelessly outdated. While talking to me Truesdell became indignant but I was not surprised since Grattan-Guinness, in spite of my warning, published a few superficial items by the ignorant Porter (§ 15.1) in his *Companion Enc. of the History and Philosophy of the Math. Sciences* of 1994. Grattan-Guinness had indeed understood the general tendency of neglecting rigour, see my *Black Book* (2017b).

14.4. The window abroad began to close gradually. Instead of Youshkevich three other people had to approve a publication abroad, the director, Party secretary and the trade union head of the appropriate institution. Then that privilege was only left for academic institutions (with practically non-existing exceptions) and finally those institutions were forbidden to accept manuscripts from outsiders (whom I was for the Inst. Hist.). Another possibility appeared instead: the Agency mentioned in § 11.7, was established, as though a Foreign Office for authors and translators. Academic institutions, but hardly any other establishments, could submit them the manuscripts even of outsiders, but in Russian, to be checked against any inappropriateness.

So I began to compile my manuscripts in Russian and to translate them during such checks. Two circumstances appeared at once. First, a translation was decidedly worse than that same text if originally written in English. Second, some corrections and often additions seemed necessary, i. e., *transgressions* became unavoidable. At first, they remained unnoticed, but then one of my manuscripts was rejected. I think that *they* could have even banned me forever.

An American colleague then in Moscow, Dauben, had smuggled that manuscript out of the country and Truesdell published it. An English colleague read its proofs (but missed five or six misprints). In all, Truesdell had published 29 of my manuscripts, a record for him and me, and two more appeared in the *Archive* after he had quitted.

A similar case: in 1975, the International Statistical Institute (ISI) held a session in Warsaw and I somehow became able to send there the text of my invited report. It had to be approved by the editor in England, but the Poles refused to send him my unofficially received text. So I sent that editor about ten trifling letters with pages of my report written in pencil on the other sides of the pages. He soon understood my intention but had to arrange the typing of my real text. He had to ask the Poles insistently before they sent him my typed text (1975). Did anyone abroad have even an inkling of such doings? To come personally to Warsaw? I did not even dream of such a possibility.

I was elected to the ISI in 1975 and am sure that that helped me to hold out in our Institute. It is opportune to add however that that scientific body, as likely most scientific societies had deteriorated owing to lack of money and the need to admit almost anyone, see my booklet (2017b). And since it is not anymore interested in the history of statistics, I quit it.

14.5. The same rules applied at the Agency for comparatively very short abstracts which I had been compiling for the *Zentralblatt für Mathematik* (now, *Zentralblatt MATH*). They had been sending me copies of papers and books for the reviewing. Two copies of Pearson (1978) with subtitle *Against the Background of* [...] *and Religious Thought* disappeared one after the other. I understand that a third copy had been sent by registered mail (my advice) and returned to the sender.

But what could we do with the wretched leftovers of the currency that we finally got from the Agency (which grabbed the lion's share of our royalties)? In Moscow, several stores of Beriozka (little Birches) were opened and sold oversea goods for currencies. Currencies? No, certainly not. At least we, authors and translators, never saw them. Instead, we got certificates. A bus ticket is a certificate, it ensures the right to go somewhere on the bus. In Moscow at that time, it was understood in a narrow sense: it ensured the right to buy goods in the Beriozka stores. At once, new black market operations began, two *usual* roubles were offered for a *certificate rouble* although such operations fell under a strict article of the Penal Code and in spite of the worsening of the choice of the goods. Indeed, the government, invariably at the lookout for currencies, took a great deal of them earmarked for Beriozka (information from a reliable source).

14.6. Here is a real story about a young son of my relatives. His parents gave him some certificates, he bought a pair of shoes, at once sold them for *usual* roubles but was apprehended. Note: he diligently sold the shoes rather than the certificates and thus avoided the much stricter article of the Penal Code. Nevertheless, normally he would have been sent *to the chemistry* (to work for, say, six months outside Moscow in some enterprise, for example, in a chemical plant) and never obtain the required anew right of residence in Moscow. Some strings were pulled and some bribes were apparently given, and he escaped with a mildest sentence: a fine of 300 roubles. This is an illustration of an ugliest side of our *happy* existence. And one more remark: the militia thus easily fulfilled their quota of successive work (everything was planned!) so did it have a possibility or a wish to hunt down much more evasive real economic offenders?

15. The International Academy

15.1. For a long time I kept thinking of leaving the International Academy of History of Science, Intern. Acad., just as I left the ISI
(§ 14.4) because it became invaded by ignoramuses as well. One of them, T M. Porter, stated that *Even mathematicians cannot prove the fourth dimension,* see Sheynin (2006a) (and, in addition, since the editor of its *Archives* actually impeded the publication of materials describing events after the mid-18th century. Happily, he left). Once, after becoming an effective member (§ 15.3), I even received materials for voting with a request: *elect not less than* … I refused to vote.

To explain. National academies do not admit historians of science (a practice which I consider utterly wrong), so by the end of the 19th century they, those historians, got together and established that Academy. Until recently, it remained highly prestigious. An example: In 1990, when being in Paris (§ 20.4), I was its corresponding member. An eminent French historian of science called me *Professor*, and I pointed out his mistake. – *As a member of the Academy, you are more than professor.*

So, about 1980 I asked Truesdell to recommend me for election. He agreed, but expressed his low opinion about that body. In my own words: he considered it as a loose union of individuals whereas I still cherished it and badly needed a support for remaining in the Institute.

15.2. I was included in the list of candidates for election but only after successfully sending them a completed questionnaire about myself. At first, it did not arrive but I sent them another letter by a devious way.

A scandal! He dared to think about election! And who is he, anyway? Even Youshkevich was questioned: why did he communicate his manuscripts?

Because they were worthy, and the following does not concern me.

Gribanov, an instructor of the Central Committee of our great Party, called me. He asked me to withdraw my candidature.

We have worthier scientists, Gnedenko and (who do you think?) *Maistrov who are not candidates.*

Gnedenko, a scholar *with a divine spark* (Youshkevich). But he either became exhausted or lost interest in real science. I have read his joint popular booklet (Gnedenko & Khinchin 1946 and many later editions). Khinchin died in 1959, so its merits are mostly his. Vile trash, almost on the level of Baron Munchausen. An English translation of that booklet published in 1961 became dated (Gnedenko had since added new material), lacked commentaries, and therefore rendered a bad service to its readers.

As a historian, he had published worthy work on Russian scientists but at the end of his life (he died in 1995) he published an essay on the history of probability dated by about 30 years. He is not known abroad as a historian and Bolshev told me that he did not consider Gnedenko as a historian either.

About 1989 an able mathematician whose name I regrettably forgot told me in Moscow that Gnedenko is not enjoying authority (anymore). Kolmogorov, as he added, gave him a letter in an open envelope for another mathematician. An open envelope meant that Kolmogorov wished to disclose the essence of his letter. That is how that able mathematician understood the situation and read the letter. Kolmogorov advised the addressee (unsuccessfully) to recommend Gnedenko's transfer to the Siberian branch of the Academy; *otherwise we will not get rid of him.* Indeed, it was difficult to get rid of an academician even of a republican (Ukrainian) academy. See also § 19.1.

And Maistrov? He published two only marginally interesting books. The first of them (1967) was translated into English in 1974 since at that time there did not exist any other book on the history of probability; Todhunter (1865) was the only exception. In his second book (1980) he plagiarized me. I ought to add that Maistrov had other interests as well; for example, he published a book on the history of computing devices which I cannot judge. He was a petty philosopher and a poor mathematician, superficially discussed the struggle of materialism with idealism and barely knew German but no other foreign language at all.

I asked Gribanov (perhaps in an excited voice) whether he knew that I had been ousted from the Institute. At first he *did not understand* me, then told me that he did not know anything about it. Gribanov later disgustedly told someone at the Institute that I had shouted at him. At the Institute, I had accidently seen an everyday order in which some students including a certain Gribanov were officially thanked for some amateur performances. Youshkevich later enlightened me:

Our director (Mikulinsky, a corresponding member of the national Academy of Sciences) *approaches him on tiptoes.*

15.3. A queer real story about Mikulinsky. He was a Jew, but in 1941 or a bit earlier, when receiving his first passport, he called himself Russian. Such practice was allowed then. However, in the 1970s his pestering began. How dared he? After some time that campaign against him petered out, but he was obliged to call himself a Jew in Party documents. That demand was withdrawn, again after some time.

In the artillery school, just before graduation, we were allowed (unofficially?) to change our name and/or nationality. I did not use this opportunity, but our Eisenberg became Eisenbergas. He was not Jewish in appearance and his mother was possibly Lithuanian.

The votes at the Academy could be casted by letter and Soviet members, apparently all of them from the Inst. Hist., left their votes *in open envelopes* in the office of that institute. Youshkevich, however, often went abroad and took pains to vote while there. One of those members, A. T. Grigorian, even (unsuccessfully) demanded that the Academy itself ought to withdraw my candidature since the Soviet members were against him. In 1990 Soviet members suddenly changed their opinion and that same Grigorian declared that he will vote for me! I became a corresponding member and an effective member in 1995.

16. I became interesting for the officialdom

16.1. At the end of the 1980s A. I. Volodarsky, a specialist in the history of mathematics in ancient India, but an ignoramus in my subject (and narrow-minded in general) suddenly attempted to convince me in that Maistrov's second book (1980) was important. Without any arriere-pensee? A colleague later advised me to avoid any *doubtful* matters in his presence. He was officially important: several times went abroad as a scientific secretary (!) of Soviet members at some conferences. That serious activity was officially recognized as scientific work …

In 1991, lacking any serious merits, he became corresponding member of the Academy. Dauben, whom I met in Moscow (§ 14.4), told me that Volodarsky had stated that there were no gays in the Soviet Union. *How do you know? – There are none in our Institute.* He obviously (and most clumsily) fulfilled his duty and just as obviously had more zeal than sense.

16.2. Again at the end of the 1980s a producer from the Moscow film studio called me. He needed illustrations to a film about games of chance (i. e., about the history of probability) and got my telephone number from Rosenfeld (see below). He came, began to question me and somehow mentioned the work of Maistrov. I understood soon enough that he came to have a look at a person who dared to become a candidate for election at the Academy without the blessing of the High House (which I mentioned in § 10.9). He called me the next day and asked my opinion about the Bayes theorem, wished to make it absolutely clear who he was. I answered mildly that his question was too difficult to answer right away.

Rosenfeld was an eminent geometrician and an expert on the Arabic mathematics (he learned Arabic). Volodarsky described him as a chatterbox (who kept silent about that *producer*), extremely negligent in his work and therefore barely tolerated by Youshkevich (and a womanizer). He moved to the US, continued to work there and died there.

I cannot say for sure whether he was an informer but I often asked myself: how many are there? In 1946, I met my fellow school student Yura Rosenberg who later became Bormotov (the name of his mother). He retold me the answer to the same question given him by his childhood friend who had been working *there*:

Look: two men in the street are selling cabbage, so one of them is certainly ours.

Horrible!

17. Our dear Party

17.1. It is time to say: I was a candidate member of the Party from 1946. It was extremely difficult for an officer to remain outside and I did not understand properly what's what and later became an effective Party member. But I was ousted from the Institute and for five years, from

1980 to 1985, until becoming an old age pensioner (men received pensions after age 60, women, after 55; one of the positive sides of the Soviet system), I remained jobless.

During those years I have written a few letters to the regional Party committee and even to the very top. They did not help me as I knew beforehand; I only wished to safeguard myself against accusations of being satisfied with doing nothing officially and probably indulging in private tutoring (I did not, see § 18.1).

Once monthly I came to the Institute to pay the dues: as jobless, 2 kopecks (and 10 kopecks more for travelling). I was repeatedly warned about my responsibility for violating the Party statutes and criticized in absentia at faculty Party meetings (but complimented for regular payment of dues). They never thought of helping me, only about my absence at the meetings, whereas I always answered: my main duty is work, and being jobless it is senseless for me to come to the meetings. Nothing happened possibly because of my international connections. A jobless person expelled from the Party and living in Moscow? My life would have been precarious. In any case I had certainly deserved to be entered in the Guinness book of records: a Party member five years detached from it, from *the mind, honour and conscience of our epoch*!

17.2. I reached 60 and just in time took my leave of the Institute's Party organization: they finally decided to take resolute steps against me. I went to the regional Party committee and asked to be transferred to a local Party organization of pensioners. They found out at once that for five years I had been jobless and looked at me detestably.

My new Party organization only asked me to pay my dues, but about 1989 I threw away my Party membership card. A call from the secretary:

You have not paid your dues. – I will not pay anymore. – Then give us your card. She was not surprised! *– I threw it away. – You should have notified us. Take me to court.*

A second call from another member of some standing in my (previous!) organization:

Why have you left? – Jobless for five years, isn't that enough? – But why did this happen? – Because I am a Jew,

as though she did not understand that. She asked permission to come for a talk, but I refused to budge. I recall a similar former question of a Russian colleague which also seemed strange to me.

You haven't liked the advice of an American sailor to move to the US (§ 6.5), *so why you did you become hostile to the pronoun* <u>*us*</u>

(§ 11.4)? *– Just make yourself up and try to find a job as* <u>*Rabinovitch*</u>.

17.3. But in 1969 I was even elected to the faculty Party bureau (I had no valid reason for declining). The Bureau usually sat at the head of Party meetings as the presidium, but I had twice tacitly remained on the floor, then reprimanded by someone.

I also recall a meeting of a small Party group, perhaps still in the laboratory of the Institute. Abalkin himself (see §§ 13.11, 17.4, 17.5) came to head it. We had to discuss a *personal case* of one of us (a relative of the eminent historian of mathematics, I. K. Andronov). He wilfully left his job in Moscow for a few days and returned with a broken leg. I timidly remarked that the leg perhaps was a sufficient penalty, but no! a leg is a private circumstance and has no connection with the Party, with our helmsman. *The great unbending Party pledged otherwise* (Mayakovsky)! A severe Party penalty was inflicted on him. I happened to hear that soon afterwards that man had killed himself, certainly not because of the penalty: he was not quite normal.

Party penalties had to be seriously reckoned with. They could have been annulled after some time if the guilty person zealously fulfilled Party assignments. Until then promotion or successful transfer to another job were hardly possible. Such assignments were either almost *neutral* (for example, checking the proper payment of dues by members in another faculty), and I attempted to restrict my duties to them, but the emphasis was on ideology: explain some Party decisions to the students, agitate *for a single candidate* during an election campaign.

A story. Brezhnev visits a market, sees an Uzbek selling a water melon.

Is there any choice? – Choose! – What can I choose? – And whom can we choose in an election?

17.4. Yes, the Party was unbending and therefore disintegrated, but Abalkin and his ilk proved quite bendable and able to straighten themselves anew, to resemble a Möbius strip.

Gorbachev was unable to bend the Party which was patently impossible. The state as a whole should have been reconstructed which was all the more impossible. Its disintegration was inevitable and I refuse to agree that that process was a disaster, much less the disaster of the century (Putin).

A few stories illustrating ordinary difficulties and successes of the perestroika. A private greengrocer's opened in Moscow and the city administration did not know how to deal with it. An inspector came there.

Why do you change prices during the day? – And why not? – The cashier is perhaps cheating. How will you know? – She is my grandmother.

A public toilet (too few of them existed) in the centre of Moscow was leased to a private person who promptly converted it into a beer cellar. The contract had not prevented any changes!

A maritime city in the Far East had been rolling in sawdust from local sawmills. A man described his activities in a newspaper article. He managed to hire beachcombers for loading a ship with sawdust and sold it in Japan. Previously, no one in the city administration thought about Japan since foreign trade was monopolized by the state.

That man, Tarasov, became the first Soviet legal millionaire (perhaps after later transactions). He was a communist, had to pay Party dues. Once he had to pay monthly dues exceeding the yearly salary of the woman who collected them. Imagine her feelings: a millionaire being a member of the Party of the working people!

In Russia, quite recently another millionaire ran for election as President. He was backed by the (new pocket) Communist party with an obvious aim: not to win the elections (naturally won by Putin by the vote of millions of people not bothering to think properly) but to show the Communist flag.

17.5. Here is Gorbachev's referendum of 1991 as described in Wikipedia. The question:

Do you consider necessary the preservation of the [USSR] *as a renewed federation of equal sovereign republics in which the rights and freedom of an individual will be fully guarantied*?

Castles in the air! Why not add

and you will become a marshal/a wife of a marshal? *Another tune will be heard, forests and mountains will join the dance*! (Krylov's fable *The Quartet*, four animals with no ear for music).

And here are the results. Participated 79.4% of those eligible of whom 76.4% answered positively. However, the Baltic, Georgia and Armenia conducted their own referendums at which overwhelming majorities voted for full independence, Moldavia was split and Kazakhstan and the Ukraine changed the question. And how about Western Ukraine? Unknown. About ten years previously one of the highest Party functionary in the Ukraine read a report in Russian and a friend, who later became a commentator of radio *Liberty* and described this episode asked him *why in Russian*?

If I steal a million my friends will possibly save me from prison, but after a report in Ukrainian I would have immediately disappeared.

The referendum was actually supported by the quite democratic constitution of 1989 which granted the union republics the right to establish diplomatic and trade relations with other countries. Apparently however, many republics were sick and tired with the Soviet Union and Soviet socialism.

The disintegration of the USSR became inevitable, could not have been prevented even *by blood and iron*. That method was indeed applied in the Baltic although on a small scale: *only* twelve people were shot. The political results were opposite to those expected by those unbendable who had *learned nothing and forgotten nothing*.

Here is a remark made about 1995 by a high-ranking Kazakhstan official in a talk with a Russian Jew: he held a high position in Moscow,

but all the same they thought that I was a chock and you were a Zhid muzzle.

An exit of a republic from the Union? That possibility was envisaged from the very beginning but only in 1990 a pertinent law was promulgated. It required a six-year period for an actual withdrawal and that same Abalkin had been specifying the necessary procedures. Too late! The USSR expired.

17.6. And here is a barely remembered episode. In 1936, on the eve of the Big Terror, the Eighth Extraordinary Congress of Soviets adopted the Stalin, and the most democratic in the whole world constitution. A report about it and about the suggested corrections was made by HIM himself. He agreed that the military service was a duty rather than a corvée and decided that some other small points were admissible. However, he refused to transform the German autonomous republic into a union republic (equal for example to the Ukraine). Yes, that autonomy excels in each important way … (he named a union republic in Central Asia, mentioned by the leaders of the German autonomy, but I forgot which one exactly), but it has nowhere to exit, it is surrounded by the Russian Federation. He recalled the non-existing possibility!

The future of that autonomy was tragic. In 1941, its population was banished to Siberia and Kazakhstan and *unnecessarily* lived there in an extremely restrained way. After Stalin's death they were allowed to return and their autonomy was promised to be announced as well. Then, however, Putin annulled that promise. Many Germans lost their native tongue, became Russified in a bad sense.

Also on the eve of the Big Terror Lebedev-Kumach, one of the leading Soviet poets, compiled a song which contained a line

Life became better, life became merrier

and Stalin repeated it with a single new word: *Life became better, comrades*, … And then the Big Terror (sorry! The Great Merriment) began.

18. My family

18.1. During those jobless years I intensively continued my scientific work, published five papers in the *Archive* (1980 – 1985) on the history of the statistical method in various branches of natural sciences, and even tacitly thanked Mochalov for such a possibility.

It is time to say also that I married in 1957. My late wife Ida, née Blostein, did not pester me. She understood that for me a job was impossible. After being kicked out of the Institute, pedagogic work was not even imaginable and in addition history of mathematics was almost unneeded. And for a Party member of my standing an ordinary job (to put it bluntly, as a watchman) was impossible whereas a smaller salary would have lessened my forthcoming pension (a corollary of the existing rules).

Ida never squandered money, we had some savings and I inherited some money after Father's death. Ida quit her post box at my insistence: in spite of her being remote from any secrets: her place of work could have well prevented our possible emigration. She started working somewhere else, earned less but drew her pension. We remained afloat.

In her childhood with an other-wordly mother and two elder sisters she almost hungered. Her father was pestered by the authorities and died early. He was deprived of electoral right which meant: *an undesirable element.* He could have been banished from Moscow with family. Thousands of the inhabitants of the capital were banished due not only to quite unnecessary and extremely cruel political goals but because of overcrowding. Building new houses was much more difficult! The usual Stalinist way of ruling … Much later, as I heard, plank beds appeared in many flats for people to sleep one on top of another.

Ida's father wrote a letter to Gorky, asked him to intercede. I only know that the family had remained in Moscow. In 1989 Ida became an Adventist. (Neither of us had any connection with Jewish life.) I came to know some of them, quite worthy people knowledgeable in religion and ancient history. They told a Moscow Jew: *Join us and become twice chosen*!

18.2. This statement however contradicted the opinion of another Adventist, a physician by profession, who explained to a few of other Adventists and me, that after the death of Jesus, Christians became the chosen people: the curtain in the temple was suddenly torn and some other impossible events happened. Now, I would have denied his argument. First, the Muslims had or have the custom of tearing their clothes (along the seams?) when some relative dies. Second, and extremely important: the statement of the Pope, Franzisk I. Justifying himself by Apostle Paul's *Letter to the Romans*, 11:29

For the gifts and the call of God are irrevocable,

he declared that Jews are forever the chosen people. Later he added: Christians are also chosen although that unification cannot be explained by mortals.

Here in Germany Ida began to go to a synagogue, but the language barrier proved an insurmountable obstacle. She came to the Mormons, quite worthy people like the Adventists in Moscow. Later she left them after no one defended her when another Mormon cruelly joked at her expense. Her next and last fold was *Jews for Jesus*. Contrary to the Christian tradition, Jesus as shown in the *New Testament* is abominable, but my information about it proved useless (and a few deeply religious Christians just did not want to discuss my opinion). How many times I recalled Markov (Sheynin 1993, p. 200) and generalized his statement of 1915 (he only mentioned seminarians):

A seminarian must subordinate his mind to the indications of the Holy Fathers and replace it by the texts from the Scripture.

Perhaps twenty Jews joined the Berlin branch of that sect whose language was Russian. The Community knew it but at least in those times did nothing.

18.3. Ida died in 2004. At first, she rather easily managed to survive breast cancer but for five years had to take a preventive medicine. After three years the side effects became extremely unpleasant and her doctor allowed her to quit taking it. She should have only allowed a brief respite if at all. I did not contradict her, perhaps because I never argued with Ida. Cancer one more, this time inoperable! *Never trust kind doctors*! Their kindness can disguise ignorance.

From 1999, after an operation in Cologne, Ida had been living with an artificial mitral valve. In Russia, such operations had then been hardly possible.

I myself barely survived after believing a general statement. *Never believe them*, because you can be an exception. I overheard the statement of a doctor:

No, not appendicitis. You would have felt it at once.

Well, I only felt something unpleasant and possibly only at the last minute decided to poke my finger in the proper place.

Ida was barely educated and likely afraid lest I begin to show my superiority (which I never did). She also warned me beforehand that everything should be done according to her wishes with which I readily agreed since she had enough common sense and was, unlike me, sociable. After her death her woman friend recalled to me her words: she would have been unable to remain married for a long time to anyone except me. I never heard anything similar from her! Once she complained: I was not gentle with her. – *I am unable to be gentle with my boss*. My boss she remained …

18.4. In Moscow, I underwent an adenoma surgery and, while in hospital, met a lively and pleasant Jew, a former chief mechanic of the atomic-powered icebreaker *Lenin*. About five years previously he underwent the same surgery but something went wrong and he had to come back yearly for some unpleasant treatment. I tried to speak with him in a sea language:

You are drifting now for a long time, will possibly become pinned against a rock. Why not emigrate? Perhaps you will be healed abroad. – Inconvenient. I am a participant [of WWII]. – *Aren't they participants? – I'll discuss it with my family.*

A patriotic Jew in 1989! I lost my fatherland and shed my patriotism in my student years at the Geodetic Institute since state antisemitism became evident. Thus, a Jewish student told me that a group of students of a military academy including him, all of them Jews, were expelled due to an alleged poor performance which was a damned lie.

18.5. My son Michael came here without knowing a single German word, but he managed to master it in a practical way and became a successful businessman. I am sure that he treated us, his parents, later me alone, better than an overwhelming majority of other sons or daughters. Here is a failed American saying:

A son is a son until he takes a wife,
A daughter is a daughter all her life.

Without his financial aid my scientific work would have ended and I myself would have found myself in a deplorable state. I have to pay for some medicines which become more costly and more numerous with time (the number of free medicines diminishes). An orthopaedist healed my *plantar fascitis*, pain in the heel but for three procedures I had to pay 258 Euros (the cost nowadays is possibly much lower).

About 2010 two German physicians published a newspaper letter. They suggested to deny to people over age 75 any medical help except for prescribing them painkillers. Negative commentaries followed but the authors had warned that they will not participate in any discussions. Their suggestion was certainly forgotten, but something similar is happening. A yearly urological blood analysis was only free until age 80, after which I had to pay for it. I recall that Father, when entering his last hospital decreased his age by nine years: *otherwise they will not treat me properly*. Old patients are likely everywhere treated rather carelessly.

Some peculiarity of my heart compelled me to quit a short-lived attempt at weight lifting; even badminton with its variable stress became impossible. Instead, I began jogging when many Russians still regarded that practice as a lunacy of sorts. Jogged day in and day out, 365 times yearly, 40 minutes daily, for about 40 years until age 77. Then, instead, started walking rapidly about 75 minutes daily, am still walking, rapidly but much slower, am working out about 55 minutes daily, at 92 + am able to continue my scientific work (and to compile this essay).

My grandson Aleksandr came here at the ripe old age of four. Went to a kindergarten for a few days, then declared:

I will continue after all the children learned Russian.

Nevertheless, as expected, he got acquainted and I asked him whether he likes his life here.

Yes, I go to the kindergarten and get pocket money.

German became his first language, but his (Moscow) Russian is almost perfect, without any foreign accent. For two years he studied in a boarding school in England, graduated here from a gymnasium, then from some economic educational institution, became a successful businessman as his father (as my son).

19. Science once more

19.1. A chapter on the theory of probability had to be included in the intended monograph on mathematics of the 19th century. Youshkevich asked Gnedenko to compile it but he required my participation. Then I was asked but I required a participation of a modern mathematician. We were united and I wrote a draft of almost everything needed. I naturally based the section describing the work of Chebyshev, Markov and Lyapunov on Gnedenko's contributions.

He checked my work and compiled an Introduction and Conclusion. He singled out a phrase which pleased him, but I told him that it was his own phrase written about twenty years ago. Our text went to Kolmogorov, who was one of the two editors. He revealed a few mistakes which I made and which Gnedenko had missed and unjustly deleted my description of the Dirac delta function as derived by Laplace. I later understood my mistake: I had not noticed that an occurring multiple integral did not exist in the language of generalized functions. Kolmogorov could have added: *but for his time Laplace's considerations were remarkable*. At times, geniuses are apparently too resolute.

Gnedenko servilely agreed with each decision made by Kolmogorov, then Youshkevich added some material and somewhat corrected us. I had previously reported that investigation of Laplace at the University seminar and only Rosenfeld noticed my mistake whereas Youshkevich decided that everything was understandable. Rosenfeld did not object and other participants were silent. Rosenfeld told me once that, had it been in Youshkevich's power, I

would have long ago become doctor of science. He himself, however, insistently attempted to diminish me in Youshkevich' eyes. And I did not forget his dirty participation in absentia in the episode with the producer
(§ 16.2).

19.2. I translated a paper by Youshkevich and Rosenfeld (1996) and Yoshkevich as Rosenfeld told me asked me to delete my name. Perhaps a paper for an Arabic source prepared by three Jews would insult the Arabs? That was my feeling. Their text was submitted previously after being translated by someone else but rejected as hardly understandable. I had not bothered to translate a rare geometric term since Rosenfeld would be able to do it at once. He was indeed able, but told Youshkevich: *Sheynin did not know this term.*

Gnedenko treated me ambiguously. He knew that my position at the Plekhanov Institute became uncertain and compiled a reference for me (which I had not used because of some stupid idea) and gave me Kolmogorov's telephone number. Kolmogorov however did not respond. Told me that before helping it would be necessary to study some documents and hung up on me.

On the other hand, Gnedenko attempted to misappropriate the entire royalty due us and a colleague told me that that attempt was not the first one. Gnedenko wished me to continue my collaboration but I evaded him. Why collaborate with someone who does not notice my mistakes? And the failed attempt mentioned above added to my misgivings. Youshkevich tried to convince me but to no avail and I heard his comment: my refusal will harm Gnedenko more than me.

Translations of the few volumes of the monograph on history of mathematics had appeared gradually; in § 11.7 I described the difficulties which occurred when *my* volume was being translated.

20. Paris

20.1 In 1990 French statisticians invited me, already a corresponding member of the International Academy, to come to Paris and report about my work. My son Michael managed to obtain foreign passports for me and Ida. My name was written (and still officially is) in an ugly manner, as an illiterate mix of German and French: OsKar Cheinine!

Foreign travels became simpler: new times under Andropov, a democrat … A story. An elderly Jew living in Moscow blurted out something inappropriate. His *crime* became known and he was summoned to come with his passport to the dreaded Liubianka street, the headquarters of the KGB. He came, gave up his passport at the entrance and was directed to a certain official. He was thoroughly reprimanded and tearfully begged to be excused. Went home delighted by the absence of punishment and was visited next day by the district militia officer.

Why are you living without registration? – Oh, but I am living here for many years. – Your passport! And there it was: *Departed*! *– Leave Moscow in 24 hours or else.*

An elderly man was thrown out of home and probably without any close relatives elsewhere. New times, Andropov, the democrat! But certainly, as compared with the Devil Incarnate … My second thought: at the last moment the *criminal* was perhaps pardoned. But even then his moral punishment would have been much too cruel all the more so since he only was a criminal from the criminal Bolshevik viewpoint.

20.2. Now I had to go the French consulate for the visas. But where is it? The official information booths were helpless: Soviet citizens to not visit foreign consulates! Go to the Ministry of Foreign Affairs where they will be happy to help … Hardly. But such information became readily available from private booths, and I succeeded.

Paris! We walked the streets. Boulevard Saint-Michel, the Eiffel Tower … Ida was in the seventh heaven. Who of her friends or relatives thought of being *really* abroad, not even in Bulgaria or Poland? Did she even dream of such a marvel?

Chkalov, a pilot who was the first to fly to America non-stop and became a national hero, was asked there what he was feeling. He allegedly answered: *I yearn for my fatherland.* Chkalov perished in the air when something happened with his plane. I heard that he insistently asked Stalin to stop the terror … And it was impossible to arrest a national hero.

I had a yearning for my desk the more so since we saw Muslims openly urinating in underground passages.

20.3. Europe had taken in millions of Muslims whereas even the richest Muslim countries did nothing. The distorted idea of freedom allows such vulgarity (and disturbance of public hygiene) as mentioned above. Much more: verdicts contravening common sense are being reached at least in the US and their beneficiaries are even awarded *Shnobel prizes*! A thief entered the garage of his victim, was unable to enter his house or for some reason even to escape. Remained in the garage two or three days and was awarded damages to the tune of ten thousand dollars …

European Muslims openly declare that they will enslave the continent. Freedom of speech in the Shnobel sense! See § 4.2. Iran declares that it will destroy Israel. Intended genocide? No, the same freedom. Democracy in the usual sense is dead and no ersatz is visible. Mankind will either change or degenerate if not annihilate itself by a crazy nuclear war. Change, however, will hardly happen.

Thus, after two thousand years hundreds of millions of Christian still believe that Judas had betrayed Jesus. Actually, betrayed when being hypnotized by the Devil, who had entered him (John 13:2), betrayed after Jesus urged him to go the Romans promptly (John 13:27).

In the eyes of believers (to whom I do not belong) that Muslim invasion of Europe can be seen as a divine retribution for, or agreement with the annihilation of the European Jewry. However, I ought to add: we are not blameless either, see end of § 24.1. And in § 24.3 I mention my manuscript in which Dostoevsky is quoted. He did time for political activity which was only criminal in the eyes of a dictatorship and noted that Jewish inmates largely kept aloof, and as though felt disgust for the Russian nation. Much later, possibly not quite normal after prison, Dostoevsky became blatantly anti-Semitic (Ibidem).

20.4. In Paris, I read two reports in English. A remarkable Englishman, Bill Farebrother, a statistician and an able mathematician came to Paris with his wife, Sheila, and was present at one of my reports. Asked me something and I answered:

Until this minute I thought I understand English.

The French began tittering and Bill was embarrassed. He, a Liverpudlian, apparently spoke at home with the local accent and had to repeat his question in ordinary English. An American who then was in Paris told me that he understood that local English but only since he lived there for some time.

Both Bill and Sheila intended to visit Paris and had come to see me as well since we had previously corresponded. A hereditary illness or syndrome gradually blinded him and he was almost blind. What a waste! Later they visited us in Cologne. Still later he acquired a guide dog and asked my permission to call him *Oscar*. I agreed and received a large photo of my namesake, of a very good-looking dog.

A story. Father speaks with daughter.

Are you a virgin? – No. – Who is that rascal? – He is not a rascal. I forgot his name but his dog was called Voltaire.

I visited the consulates of England, the US and Canada to find out the possibility of emigration, but did not hear anything consolatory. Back in Moscow I went to the British consulate with the same aim. Spoke for a rather long time with an official, quoted Longfellow about which she knew nothing. The result: you may come if you have 200,000 pounds outside Russia. For some reason did not have such money. A former cannibal from the Mumbo-Yumbo tribe can come, but not a Russian Jew!

20.5. After managing to come to Germany we lived for free in a hotel and all day long had to hear the street noise. Some newcomers lived even on a ship tied up on the Rhine in awful conditions, sometimes having Arabs for next-door neighbours.

Then we found a flat for ourselves. Many Germans wished to occupy it, but the owner selected us *for our beautiful eyes*. I came to visit him. He spoke High German which I understood and I spoke English. Everything seemed to be arranged but next day he called our community.

That Sheynin, his English is perfect, tomorrow he will go to England. – No, no, there will be no welfare for him.

Recall the 200,000 pounds! And we became happy. A flat on the fourth floor, no lift, stove heating, coal in the cellar. That was the beginning of our new life in Germany, in Cologne.

21. The Statistical Society

21.1. In 1991 I suddenly received a diploma of the Royal Statistical Society:

In recognition of services to statistics the President, Council and Fellows of the Society have elected Oscar Borisevich [Borisovich] *Sheynin to be an Honorary Fellow. London, 11 June 1991*

A high honour, I followed Chuprov and Kolmogorov! But I suspect that most honorary fellows are figureheads and do not participate in the life of the Society. I was never invited to contribute anything or lecture, I only published two or three letters in the Society's information bulletin.

In 2005, the journal of the Society, vol. A168, published a paper by A. Rice and E. Seneta on the work of De Morgan, a most eminent logician who also published contributions on probability. I submitted a tiny letter to that journal in which I noted that in a paper by De Morgan quoted by those authors he stated that an event having probability 2.5 occurs twice with an equal chance of its happening or failing for the third time. Rice & Seneta did not even read that paper!

The journal kept silent and in a few months I began to bother it, but only got certainly misleading answers:

The authors apparently (!) *had not yet answered your letter …*

I wrote to the President, but he never answered. I demanded a definite answer from the Editor and got a rudely formulated and senselessly motivated answer: my letter was rejected. I quit the Society which does not allow any criticism of its publications (as I understood only then) and humiliates its honorary fellows. Did any other honorary fellow leave the Society during its 165 years of existence (ca. 1840 – 2005)? Hardly.

I was informed that the Council will discuss my decision whose members will certainly regret it (and shed crocodile tears) and that I am free to return at any time. Yes, I will as soon as those who humiliated me will repent which will happen just after the coming of turrets on wheels. Many years later I read the book of De Morgan's widow (1882) which contained the text of De Morgan's letter of 1842 to John Herschel (whose answer I did not find). De Morgan, the most eminent logician, indicated but not justified *unquestionable* truths (I would say, *soft-boiled boots*, as the Russian saying goes):

$$\sin\infty = 0,\ \cos\infty = 0,\ \tan\infty = \mp\sqrt{-1},\ \cot\infty = \tan\infty.$$

Quite recently I decided that those who had offended me are not holding any responsible positions anymore and returned.

22. History of statistics

22.1. I am continuing my scientific work. In the history of statistics and probability I see an unimaginable number of poorly written contributions (and mentioned a few appropriate examples in §§ 11.6 and 11.8). E. D. Sylla, a specialist in classical languages translated Jakob Bernoulli's *Ars Conjectandi* into English and I ended my review (2006b) of her work by a saying: *Cobbler, stick to you last*! Another upstart, T. M. Porter, compiled a biography of Karl Pearson (and was therefore elected effective member of the International Academy apparently since no one bothered to read it). In my review (2006a) of his work I quoted his curious, to say it politely, statements, for example:

Even mathematicians cannot prove the fourth dimension.

Another *scientist*, Yu. V. Chaikovsky, this time in Russia, invented a Cardano – Bernoulli law of large numbers. His manuscript was irresponsibly recommended for publication by Professor Albert Shiraev. I was a member of the editorial council of the pertinent journal, actually only a figurehead, and withdrew from it. And a few wise men shortened the chronology of civilization by one and a half thousand years and for a long time persuaded the Soviet Academy of Sciences into adopting it although not without the unbelievable support of that same *scientifically criminal* Shiraev and the great Party (Novikov 2000).

History of science is the home front of current studies, it digests and secures the newly conquered territories and even allows a glance ahead. From its workers it demands knowledge of languages (desirably of Latin and sometimes of Arabic not to mention Russian), a solicitous treatment of our classics and at least a general understanding of the situation in the front line. The last-mentioned requirement becomes more difficult with age and studies of the past but its fulfilment is extremely important. Indeed, even Euclid and Aristotle ought to be commented on a modern level and it is thought that each generation discovers Shakespeare anew. So, especially valuable are those historians of science who master modernity (I do not). A special feature of the history of science is that it allows its workers to continue their work longer than it is possible elsewhere.

More directly history of science is needed for compiling biographies of scientists for various reference sources and collected works and for pedagogic use: it is able to encourage students and in any case to help them realize the essence of new discoveries. A theory is known to be better understood after glancing at it from the outside. I read somewhere about a German teacher of history who went with his students to a hill outside their town and asked them: How could have our town been captured in the … century?

In the ideal case a modern scientist ought to prepare himself gradually for work in the rear, otherwise such transition is much more difficult. An example: Professor Novak (§ 13.9) once said a few words about V. P. Vetchinkin, a student of Zhukovsky, with whom he, Novak, was somehow connected. I asked him, why not compile a paper about Vetchinkin?

I would have to compare him with Zhukovsky, a delicate matter … A usual matter in history of science. Valuable testimonials are thus lost!

22.2. Joint work of a modern mathematician and a historian of mathematics can be very valuable; thus Kolmogorov and Youshkevich were the joint editors of a monograph (§§ 12 and 19). There also the joint work of Gnedenko and me was mentioned. Note however that Gnedenko published important historical work (§ 19.1) and the same is true about Kolmogorov (Demidov 2003).

I have published two other joint papers (Pfanzagl & Sheynin 1996; 1997). I discovered an interesting paper of a forgotten German mathematician, Lüroth, described it in his language and asked Pfanzagl to add a comment. So he did, but first I had to explain to him that dated language. The result was a publication (1996) in *Biometrika.*

Internet became a mighty aid, but it is dangerous. Attention is necessarily directed to the latest publications whereas previous and often reliable work is sometimes missed. Never trust Internet blindly!

I was able to discover a number of unknown facts and to compile a previously lacking monograph on the history of probability and theory of errors and, in a large part, of statistics (2017a). Todhunter (1865) is certainly still important, but naturally much dated. Those who wish can find much interesting on my website (see the very beginning of this essay). Thus, I presented a rendition of the most important pt. 4 of Jakob Bernoulli's *Ars Conjectandi* into English (Bernoulli Jakob 2005). I do not know Latin and therefore compiled a text based on the translations of that pt. 4 into Russian, German and French. It is better than any of these three sources.

23. Germany again

23.1. Michael had already moved to Germany and his friend invited me and Ida to come to Germany for a short while. He himself drew welfare and was therefore unable to invite us. His wife Galina and son Aleksandr came later. Professor Klaus Dietz with whom I corresponded had sent me a scientific invitation for reporting at a conference (as I asked him to do), and I was able to enter the German consulate in Moscow for visas; the consulate was as though besieged by Russians (and perhaps Jews) wishing to emigrate. Dietz was director of the Institute of Medical Biometry in Tübingen, and I did report there later. He was interested in the history of statistics, published a few interesting contributions but had no time for continuing. For a long time now I did not hear from Dietz and was unable to contact him.

I and Ida landed in Cologne and were admitted into the local Jewish Community; a rabbi was satisfied by our *attraction* to Judaism. Then I went to the authorities of that Land and asked permission to remain permanently.

This year we have already admitted (he mentioned some large number) *of newcomers. Our Land is not a haven. – We are members of the Cologne Jewish Community. – That's a different case.*

We spoke German (he refused to speak English (*You are in Germany*). We obtained *Duldung* (Toleration) and *social help* (welfare), lived freely in a hotel until becoming able to find a *social* (cheap enough) free flat. In a few months we were also granted permanent residence.

A Russian who escaped to the US a few decades earlier told me in ca. 1988 that an American had assured him: since he did not intend to return to Russia, he was an American. Nothing comparable exists here in Germany. However, Chuprov (2009), in a letter of 23 July 1920 from Berlin noted that the Germans were very well inclined towards Russian newcomers. They were afraid of their own Bolsheviks and *even excessively thought that we belonged to them.* That attitude reflected the situation of the time and does not exist anymore.

At least twenty years ago many Germans did not understand that Germany needs newcomers although certainly not Muslims, cf.
§ 20.2. The third and fourth generation of German Turks are now living here but they hardly mix with Germans. I read in the newspapers that young Turks were delighted to see in a Turkish film how Muslims killed Christians and Jews. And the relations of Germany with Turkey must take into account the interests of German Turks.

And so, take in Christians and Jews. Their second and certainly third generation will be almost Germans. German Jews have mightily contributed to German science and culture; suffice it to name Einstein and Heine. I also mention a barely known fact. In pre-revolutionary Russia the army consisted of Slavs and Jews; other nations living in Russia did not have to serve in the army. I see only one explanation: in spite of its antisemitism the elite understood that Jews were closer to the Slavs than any other such nation. And at least theoretically we and only we belong to the same civilization. Petr Berngardovich Struve, an economist and philosopher expressed the same idea in a newspaper letter of 1909 (Solzhenitsyn 2001/2009, vol. 1, p. 493).

23.2. The Central Council of Jews in Germany never approved emigration to Germany (Israel is the place to move to) but does not prevent it. At a certain conference a German official asked the representative of that Council why only a half of the newly arrived Jews had entered Jewish communities. That representative naturally answered that he should address that question to the consulate in Moscow, but I wish to add, first, that many of those newcomers somehow *became* Jews and second, that the *guilty* Jews were not less and perhaps more valuable to the country that the *proper* Jews.

Now, the problem about people with a Jewish father who are avoided by our Communities. I heard two explanations: the paternity of a father is not obvious (and blood analyses are not recognized) and in addition only Jewish mothers somehow transmit signals about the Tora to the embryos. All Jewish mothers or not? And are those probable signals durable? I would say: admit all such people if they feel themselves Jewish. And here is the decision of the Talmud

(Makhshirin 2[7]): an abandoned child born in a town is supposed to be a Jew if the town's population is either mostly Jewish or Jewish by half. So where is the problem of paternity or are the signals about Tora?

I deny the opinion of the ultraorthodox Jews. They do not recognize the state of Israel since it was molded by humans rather than created divinely and even believe that it should be destroyed. As the Russian saying goes, *Compel a fool to pray, he will hurt his forehead.* They belong to the subspecies *Homo regressus*.

Close to these other-earthly believers I reckon the excessively learned Professor Schöps, the former head of the Mendelsohn Centre of Study of the European Jewry. An anonymous paper of the online edition of the London *Economist* for 5 – 11 Jan. 2008 described his views. This poor fellow was complaining. Russian Jews do not know and do not wish to know Jewish rituals or customs, their cultural ikons are Dostoevsky and Chaikovsky rather than Göethe and Beethoven, the less so Mendelsohn or Heine, those Jews would have preferred to see Communities as cultural rather than religious centres and (unbelievably and horribly!) prefer chess to skat. *Economist* tacitly rejected my comment and even the *Jüdisches Berlin* reminded me about the right to speech (of which I was obviously deprived). On Dostoevsky see the English text contained in **S, G,** 84 and also mentioned in §§ 20.3 and 24.2. And had not Heine remarked that a Capuchin and a Rabbi stink the same way (*Disputation*)?

It is opportune to add that Spinoza and Heine are rejected from our life as also are the brothers Rubinstein who had to baptise and thus became able to found conservatoires in Moscow and Petersburg.

Much was new for me here, in Germany, as it also surely was for all those who came here from Russia, but certainly not new at all for anyone else, and I am only partly describing it. A foreigner came to Japan and allegedly wished to write a book about it; in a month, he decided: only a paper, and after a year dropped his plan altogether!

23.3. Some officials regarded us, *Russians*, quite humanely, others were clearly hostile. One of them remarked: *You are from Russia*! *Davai, davai*! (Go on, go on working!). This *davai, davai* I heard many times. In Cologne, a teacher (an untouchable official!) openly declared that he will never mark *the Russians* highly enough.

Another point: while being a gymnasium student in Berlin my grandson wrote down the dictated formulation of a physical law but did not understand anything. *I* [the teacher] *have crowed and the sun need not rise* (a Russian saying)!

Who had ever seen an enthused official? Bismarck is quoted as saying that Germany belonged to the officials, – still belongs. In England, everything is allowed except the forbidden, in Germany it is the opposite. (The adage continues: in France, everything is allowed, even the forbidden, in Russia even the allowed is forbidden.) How vast is the field of the activities of a German official!

Russian specialists are not valued, although sometimes this attitude is justified. A blacksmith, a factory worker from some Northern city of Russia, told me that his visit of a German plant convinced him in that his knowledge was not sufficient at all.

But we certainly knew that the Russian language is great and mighty, and perhaps not worse than all the European languages taken together! Here, however, I had second thoughts. How many words were adapted (previously, mostly from German, now, often quite unnecessarily, from English) whereas the opposite process was weak (knout, pogrom, troika, the hybrid boychik, kolkhoz, bolshie, the short-lived sputnik and otkaznik, perestroika).

I even compared the weight of the main dictionaries (English – Russian and Russian – English etc.), at best only a shaky argument, and only the French language was *worse*.

My sufficiently good English and I myself are much more respected by those who speak that language, than when I speak broken German with my horrible Russian accent. Once I avoided the payment of a fine for crossing the road under a red light by speaking English with the policeman. And English proved especially useful when I had to spend a few days in a hospital. German began to *invade* me at the expense of English so I quit any attempts to improve it, to read German (except the necessary scientific literature), or to listen to news in German.

Scientific reports are often read in English and I myself read many in several German cities. Many German periodicals had replaced their German names by English equivalents and I heard that the Germans prefer to read scientific literature published in English. Something similar is apparently going on in France since a new expression was introduced there: the *Frenglish* language.

In a small town the newly arrived Jews had been housed in a certain building but then they were told that they will be housed in another town and that the just arrived buses are waiting for them. Most Jews became afraid of moving somewhere and remained. Only next morning they were told to leave the building and move to that other town on their own!

The officials had sent home a young Russian German. He lived jobless in a village near his uncle and helped him to reconstruct his house.

You have been working without a permit whereas many are here jobless.

Some German neighbour certainly informed the authorities about such disorder! Both he/she and the official were simply stupid.

I saw a disgusting poster in the Underground. A family is happy since one daughter is Lesbian! Many gays and likely Lesbians are highly talented, but their parents are surely *unhappy*, and from a general point of view such people are harmful because they seduce straights and of course lifelong gays have no children.

Much money had been spent for teaching newcomers German but the teachers often lacked any special education and their work was barely productive. I think that newcomers ought to be warned: obtain comprehensive dictionaries (for example, German – Russian and Russian – German) and a German grammar and be prepared to spend for education about six hours at home for each hour of the lessons.

Some young people including girls do not want to work; I saw an inscription on a jacket of a girl: *Work is shit*. They dress in a special way, have a special *Mohauk haircut* and many of them have large mongrel dogs. They apparently roam the country, churches are feeding them up and kind people give them money if they sit on a pavement with an empty cup before them.

23.4. Real integration in the German society (not just finding a job) is extremely difficult. A dentist, a Russian Jew, told me that he had almost no contacts with his German colleagues. For me, the situation was quite different. Only a small number of researchers work in the history of science, and contacts are rare; incidentally, Dauben (§ 14.4) remarked that the Inst. Hist. provided a unique opportunity for contacts between researchers working in various branches of the history of science. And the late W. Kruskal, a noted statistician with whom I had corresponded, recommended me to Pfanzagl, chair of the theory of probability in Cologne.

Pfanzagl received me cordially and somehow secured me a grant. Somehow, because my age prevented it. I also was useful to him (§ 22.2). Regrettably, Kruskal mentored Stigler and did not notice that his student had slandered the memory of Gauss and Euler. I described Stigler's deeds in a downloadable pamphlet **S, G,** 31.

23.5. After my move to Berlin in 1995 I began visiting the Staatsbibliothek there. It has two buildings rather far apart; House No 2 was built in the then separate West Berlin and House No. 1 is the previous *Königliche Bibliothek.* There are at least three depositaries and books are incessantly travelling from them to both Houses and back. I am unhappy with either of their buildings. House No. 1 is actually quite new and super-modern but I experienced difficulties in finding my way in its great halls. In House No. 2 you collect your ordered literature on the ground floor and read it on the next floor above. Visits are regrettably only possible for those who subscribe for a month or a year and most people do not realize what immense riches were stored by mankind during the last few centuries.

Before the advent of the computer the catalogues in both Houses were disordered. West Germany had seen many more than *seven full years*, but apparently not enough attention was directed to the catalogues. Many cards were completed by hand, in the complicated German handwriting and some of them even followed the dated German (Prussian?) method. Thus, instead of *Mathematical Methods of Economic Investigations* I found *Methods Mathematical of Investigations Economic*. Computerised catalogues can now be read (and literature ordered) from home, but there are mistakes in those catalogues and a formalised manner of compiling them is a great nuisance. Thus, if a name of a periodical is changed at least a bit, the new name is entered as a new item. So it happened with some periodicals published by the Imperial Academy in Petersburg.

Russian and Bulgarian literature is entered in the Roman alphabet and the rule for transferring words from the Cyrillic alphabet was sometimes violated. Anyway, it is difficult to find an author whose name contains hushing sounds.

Once I received 40, if I am not mistaken, reprints of a paper published in Japan, in a country outside the European Economic Community, and had to pay for them. I refused, got 20 of them and the others were destroyed. I wrote a letter protesting against this barbarism to the appropriate Minister. No reply followed, but that horrible practice was abandoned.

The situation in Germany: at least until recently even highly qualified foreigners experienced difficulties in settling here: the street was afraid of worsened conditions of life; actually, specialists create new jobs. Muslims, however, came in great multitudes. An illustration partly explaining their higher birth rate. A Soviet specialist who worked in Afghanistan before the Soviet invasion asked an ordinary local man:

You have six children, and your wife is expecting a baby. How will you feed all of them? – Wife is separating the baked bread into six parts, and will separate it into seven parts.

About ten years ago I attended a talk by an official of the Canadian consulate about the immigration to that country. Foreigners are taken in if they satisfy certain conditions (age, education, knowledge of English), Muslims on a par with others. I spoke to him, attempted to indicate the danger of creating a third (in addition to the English and French) population, but do not know whether he (much less, *they*) heeded my warning. A telling example is the foolish decision of the late Tito, president of the former Yugoslavia, to take in some Albanian Muslims.

The separation of Kosovo with persecution of its partly Christian population and destruction of valuable Christian churches followed!

The health service is predominately secured by private practitioners many of whom are experiencing serious financial difficulties caused by high taxation (cf. the situation of a Russian hospital doctor described in § 10.10). They therefore deceive the contributory sickness funds and their patients by prescribing unnecessary procedures. Hospital doctors even prescribe unnecessary operations. A Russian visitor in a hospital overheard a talk by two (German) doctors:

I prescribed her an operation. – But she hardly needs any. – This month I have not earned enough.

The second doctor was quite satisfied.

Pirogov, the founder of military surgery and one of the founders of modern surgery in general, had been working in Germany for a few years and described abominable practices of celebrated clinical physicians and surgeons (but did not mention Russian physicians). Still, humiliation of, and danger to patients such as described above was not yet known. Progress is clearly seen, especially when the situation is compared with what existed at the time of the naïve Hippocrates. Incidentally, my contribution about Pirogov (2001) was initially rejected by a German editor who justified his decision by a ridiculous cause.

Practitioners never mention treatments uncovered by those sickness funds. A friend told me about magnetic therapy, the only escape from the wheelchair in the case of my Forrestier illness. Each therapy had to last 60 minutes although later I found out that 30 minutes (or even less) were sufficient and would have been twice cheaper. A doctor who is unable to apply some modern method of treatment, can well keep silent about it. I knew an eye doctor who performed surgical operations for cataract since he was unable to apply ultrasound. And universally, doctors barely talk with their patients. *The word*, as the first means of the doctors of antiquity, has disappeared.

The situation in Berlin had recently deteriorated, I do not know why. It became very difficult to consult physicians of many specialities. In January 2018, my family doctor decided to send me to a cardiologist and gave me a referral. I received (and rejected) an appointment for November! Now, at the end of March, I do not see anything done and I say once more (§ 11.8): *Something is rotten in the state of Denmark*! If the situation does not change mortality will soon increase.

Approximately at age 81 I passed an examination in the German language and after a few months became a German citizen, but for a long time had been unable to forget an unpleasant circumstance: for this examination I paid about 250 Euros which would have been lost in case of my failure. People aged 80 or more began later receiving citizenship if certain formal conditions were met.

The examinations were different in different Lands and even in different districts of Berlin. I was lucky: I had not been asked to describe the political structure of Germany. Some officials later thought of asking to identify the building of the Bundestag. They did not understand the situation of their country, still considered the Germans as a higher subspecies (*Deutschland über alles*). But why had I wished to become a citizen? Until that time, newcomers were given special passports, but then we were required to obtain instead passports of the countries of our origin. However, I had no wish to go to the Russian consulate.

24. The Jewish life

24.1. In Moscow, there had been no Jewish life in the family of my parents. Mother, as it seems, was indifferent both to religion and her Jewishness, Father was not religious but wished to prove his worth as a Jew (§ 1.1). In general, it was impossible to enter a synagogue (§ 7.2). Once yearly Father bought matzo in the only possible shop and only until that possibility lasted. During the Gorbachev time I bought matzo in a synagogue. To show my respect, I took off my cap which naturally disgusted those standing in line.

Here, in Germany, I and Ida, in a group of 50 Russian Jews from the Berlin Community, went for a fortnight to Israel. We lived in a nice hotel in Netanya and went on excursion trips. A rabbi talked to us about very remote (as I felt) subjects. Ida was happy, but I was often bored; I needed a scientific trip.

Our guide was wonderful and I remember some of his remarks:

I cannot say that we will be living here for 50 or 100 years more, but we will do everything possible to achieve this.

Some regard the founders of new settlements as our best citizens; others however are afraid that they are drawing trouble. Anyway, it is perfectly clear that they are strong and courageous.

After a few victorious wars it was time for peace treatises. In 2000, on the invitation of Bill Clinton, the then President of the US, Barak, the prime minister of Israel, and Arafat came there for negotiations. Clinton later commented: Quite favourable conditions were offered to Arafat. He rejected them as was his right, but I, Clinton, was surprised that he had not suggested anything instead.

Israel should have hollered for the whole world to h ear: *They reject peace*! Should have showered the Palestinians with leaflets: *You are chosen as scapegoats*! This was not done, the world turned away from Israel and the Arabs were becoming ever stronger. So what does life hold in store for us?

After a fortnight our Berlin group went home, but I and Ida remained for about a week. We went to another city to visit a Moscow friend and got into serious trouble: a general strike stopped bus travels and we experienced great difficulties in returning to the airport in Tel Aviv. For a long time most unpleasant recollections did not leave me: I heard that the strike was not needed, almost everything was already agreed. At the airport we were questioned for a long time but allowed to travel back as soon as I mentioned our Berlin group. Later I understood: people, apparently not rich at all, but travelling all by themselves, were suspicious.

For about a year I edited the Russian part of the *Jüdisches Berlin.* Not all German items were translated; we, *Russians*, were obviously somewhat lower than the *Germans*. A vigorous woman, Sveta Agronik, translated the German texts. She uttered a thousand words in a minute but was alien to literature. She was unable to understand why I replaced *mentality* by *mindset* and *adepts* by *yesmen*. She wrote *shalom* instead of the Russian *sholom* and never heard about Sholem (in Russian, Sholom) Aleichem. I correctly felt that in Russia *shalom* will replace *sholom* but thought that we in Germany ought not to overcome Russia. All these discussions tired me and I left.

The Jewish Museum in Berlin is housed in the ugliest building of the city with gun ports instead of windows. All the rooms are of an irregular form, the passage from floor to floor is difficult to find and for me the exit proved impossible. After about ten minutes of my unsuccessful attempts an employee accompanied me. Nevertheless, the crazy architect was praised by Jews of high standing: everything, including the gun ports had a special meaning.

Large space was devoted to a Jewish woman who lived a few centuries ago, dutifully kept to the Jewish customs and raised many children in the same spirit. Einstein however is only given a small corner and Feuchtwanger as though published only one book. But the main point is that German Jews are shown to have been living absolutely independently from Christians. Only such a tendency really exists and is very dangerous as one of the sources of anti-Semitism or of the Christian indifference to us. An apparently real story. A young German asks his grandfather why their generation had allowed the Holocaust. Listen to the answer: *We didn't think about it*!

24.2. A few times I and Ida spent a fortnight in a special Jewish house in Bad Kissingen. Obligatory prayers on Fridays and Saturdays some of them lasting two hours, in an unfamiliar language with an additional Russian text. Talks on a low level on petty religious matters overstressing the worth of Judaism and unjustifiably humiliating other religions. One of the lecturers stated that Israel was the only democratic country lacking a constitution. I mentioned England.

But it is a constitutional monarchy. – A parliamentary monarchy.

Female servants, all of them Russian Germans, were forbidden to speak Russian with us, which only angered me. As though we will thus easier learn German!

Our food was kosher. I added some white powder in my tee but the *chief of the regime* as I called him after the GULAG manner noticed it and became horrified! He thought that I added milk after eating some meat. He lived with his wife in the best room with board and lodging, retired at age 75 and bought a house in that city, in Bad Kissingen. Not a bad job he had, looking after the *Russians*.

Orthodox Jews obey many other restrictions as well. They cannot push the button of an electric bell, cannot open an umbrella (build a house!) or warm their food by electricity on a Saturday. Here are more important examples. An orthodox Canadian family left the door of their flat opened as required on certain days. Some impudent fellows entered and openly grabbed valuable objects. The family did not dare even to call the police although later a rabbi told them that that was allowed.

Somewhere in Russia at the end of the 18th century Cossacks burst into a Jewish settlement and killed 50 inhabitants but one Jew defending himself killed two of those knackers. Next day the rabbi declared that that brave man was only allowed to pray. The inhabitants obediently agreed with his crazy statement and stopped talking to that criminal. That man had to move to the US (and became the founder of a happy Jewish dynasty).

In that same book whose title I forgot I read: when the mass influx of Russian Jews into the US began, they experienced the most antagonistic receipt from the German Jews already acclimatized there. So much for Jewish solidarity!

In the second *ideological* Jewish house our *Russian* administrator on a Saturday pushed the button of the electric stove to warm our dinner. The rabbi brought there for a short while from Israel easily revealed this crime and told us that only our children prevented him from declaring the food non-kosher (and having it destroyed).

That rabbi smoked (*the Talmud does not forbid it*) so that his indignation was senseless. His wife, an enthusiastic fool, delivered a lecture on a low level without paying any attention to her crying baby. She told us that Judaism forbids talks with the dead but then without any comments described such a transgression.

The justification of the Orthodox Judaism is that it saved the Jewry whereas nothing was left from many other ancient nations. Yes, but what was the price? I take a neutral example. Swamps had been drained to establish Petersburg and about 10 – 12 thousand people had perished (bad water, food and clothing, malaria), so who of us, of the living, may say: *On the other hand*, ..? Only the perished have that right, but they remain silent and perhaps they would have said: *To hell with Petersburg*!

Why we were scattered across the world? We did not sin more than the other ancient nations, but God required more from His chosen people (and we paid for this distinction by millions of lives). After being dispersed, we had still been unable to comply with all the Commandments, so it was sufficient to keep to them more strictly than previously and, in the first place to defend ourselves against any attack. Again, we should have been living calmly in our new places, be friendly with our neighbours and return ourselves (thus forestalling God's care about us) as soon as we feel worthy enough.

A story. Moses speaks with God.

Ten commandments ... so many! Delete at least one, for example ... – Moses, do not bargain! – But there is no such commandment!

I published a contribution (1998) which concerned the Old Testament and the Talmud and which was previously rejected by that Schöps as Editor of his periodical. I do not remember his explanation but my work obviously did not fit into the hardly comparable items there. Here is an episode which I described (redemption of the firstborn child from those who were not redeemed by the Levites).

According to the Old Testament Moses wrote *Levite* on 22,000 ballots and 273 more ballots demanding 5 shekels. The Jerusalem Talmud however mentions 22,273 *Levite* ballots. Only 22,273 Israelites drew the ballots so that Moses ran the risk of losing some money. Nevertheless, the 273 ballots came up at regular intervals.

The extra ballots were needed since the Israelites were afraid that the last ones to vote will certainly have to pay. Now, in the late 1960s, the would-be owners-occupiers of a house under construction in Moscow had to select their future flats by lot. Similar doubts were expressed but Tutubalin (1972, § 2.1) proved that these doubts were unfounded.

24.3. I also compiled some Russian manuscripts on various Jewish matters (**S, G,** 84) although one of them is in Russian and English. Here are some of my conclusions; however, instead of deeply delving here into religion I additionally refer to the English text also contained there and entitled *We are the victims of our own religion.*

1) The Israel's elite is not morally better than the top people in other countries. Thus, Defence Minister Moshe Dayan, Israel's national hero, cowardly refused to issue written orders (Sharon 1989, p. 222). His oral orders were naturally invalid and disobeyed by everyone except Sharon and hundreds of soldiers and officers perished. Actually, he became traitor to his own country.

2) During the first years of the existence of Israel the ruling Labour Party greatly hindered economic growth by absolute denial of capitalism. The positive aspect of that attitude was that the Soviet Union hoped to see a new socialist state and voted for the recognition of Israel by the UN. Later, when the Labour Party lost many followers it concluded an agreement with two small orthodox parties who became able, contrary to the opinion of the majority of population, to prohibit the flights of passenger aircraft on Saturdays and cultivation of the land on Sabbath years.

3) The Christian tradition essentially corrupts the text of the *New Testament*. In addition to what is stated in the manuscript mentioned above I quote Luke 19:27:

But as for those enemies of mine who did not want me to be king over them bring them here and slaughter them in my presence.

Those *enemies* consisted of an overwhelming majority of Jews who did not believe that Jesus was the Son of God: he had not delivered them from the Romans. He is seen here as a most spiteful sovereign and an impostor. And the true story of Judas (§ 20.3) raises most important theological problems whose solution seems extremely difficult. It was quite easy for Christianity to say that Judas was a traitor and thus to unite Christians in the face of the enemy, the Jews.

4) The extension of Christianity was hardly possible without antisemitism. Göring, the first man after Hitler in Nazi Germany, properly remarked: had there been no Jews, they should have been invented.

Bibliography

Abbreviation: IMI = *Istoriko-Matematicheskie Issledovania*

As stated in the very beginning **S, G,** n means that the source in question is available as a downloadable file n on my website www.sheynin.de which is being diligently copied: Google, Oscar Sheynin, Home

Anonymous (1937, Russian), On the all-union census of the population. Newspaper *Izvestia*, 26 Sept. 1937.

Anonymous (1954, Russian), Survey of the scientific debates on statistics. *Vestnik Statistiki*, No. 5, pp. 39 – 95.

Anonymous (1955, Russian), On the role of the law of large numbers in statistics. *Uchenye Zapiski po Statistike*, vol. 1, pp. 153 – 165.

Bernoulli Jakob (2005), *On the Law of Large Numbers*, this being a rendition of pt. 4 of his *Ars Conjectandi* by O. Sheynin. **S, G,** 8.

Birman I. (1960, Russian), Scientific debates on the application of mathematical methods in economic investigations and planning. *Vestnik Statistiki*, No. 7, pp. 41 – 52.

Bomford G. (1952), *Geodesy*. Oxford, 1962, 1971, 1980. Russian translation by O. Sheynin: Moscow, 1958.

Buniakovsky V. Ya. (1866, Russian), Essay on the laws of mortality in Russia and on the age distribution of the orthodox population. *Zapiski Imp. Akad. Nauk*, vol. 8, Suppl. 6. Separate paging.

Chebotarev A. S. (1951, Russian), On mathematical treatment of measurements. *Trudy Mosk. Inst. Inzhenerov Geod., Aerofotos'emki i Kartografii* No. 9, pp. 3 – 16.

--- (1953), Same title. Ibidem, vol. 15, pp. 21 – 27.

--- (1958), *Sposob Naimen'shikh Kvadratov* etc. (Method of Least Squares). Moscow.

Chuprov A. A. (1919), *La décomposition du bolshevisme*. No title page. Date and place of publication (Stockholm) on last p. 16. There also A. I. Chuprov who died in 1908 is called the author. The only known copy of this booklet is in Paris, in the Bibl. Nat. France. A. A. Chuprov is generally believed to be the real author.

--- (2009), *Letters to K. N. Gulkevich, 1919 – 1921*. Berlin, 2009. Publishers, Kratz G., Wittich K., Sheynin O. **S, G,** 28.

Courtois S. et al (1997), *Le livre noire du communisme*. Paris, 1999. **S, G,** 35.

Demidov S. S. (2003, Russian), Kolmogorov as historian of mathematics. *Voprosy Istorii Estestvoznania i Tekhniki*, No. 3, pp. 88 – 94.

De Morgan Sophia Elizabeth (1882), *Memoir of Augustus De Morgan*. London.

Druzhinin N. K. (1963), *Khrestomatia po Istorii Russkoi Statistiki* (Reader on the History of Russian Statistics). Moscow.

Gnedenko B. V., Khinchin A. Ya. (1946, Russian), *Elementary Introduction to the Theory of Probability*. Berlin, 2015. Translated by O. Sheynin. Many other Russian editions. **S, G,** 65.

Gorky M. (1922), *O Russkom Krestianstve* (On Russian Peasantry). Berlin.

Grodzensky S. Ya. (1987, Russian), *A. A. Markov*. Moscow.

Gumbel E. J. (1927), Vom Russland der Gegenwart. In *Auf der Suche nach Wahrheit. Ausgew. Schriften*. Berlin, 1991.

Hristov B. K. (1946, Bulg.), *Koordinaty Gaussa – Kriugera na Ellipsoide Vrashchenia* (Gauss – Krüger Coordinates on the Surface of a Rotation Ellipsoid). Moscow, 1957. Translated by O. Sheynin.

Idelson N. I. (1947), *Sposob Naimen'shikh Kvadratov* etc. (Method of Least Squares). Moscow.

Kantorovich L. V. (1959, Russian), Statement from the floor at the yearly meeting of the Academy of Sciences. *Vestnik Akad. Nauk*, vol. 29, No. 4, pp. 59 – 61.

Koetsier T., Berman L. (2005). *Mathematics and the Divine*. Amsterdam.

Kolmogorov A N., Youshkevich A. P., Editors (1978, Russian), *Mathematics of the 19th Century*, vol. 1. Basel, 1992, 2001.

Kotz S., Johnson N. L., Editors (2006), *Enc. of Statistical Sciences*, vols. 1 – 16 with single paging. Hobokan, NJ. First edition, 1982 – 1989.

Maistrov L. E. (1967, Russian), *Probability Theory. Historical Essay*. New York – London, 1974.

--- (1980), *Razvitie Poniatia Veroiatnosti* (Development of the Notion of Probability). Moscow.

Novikov S. P. (1995, Russian), Mathematicians and physicists of the Academy in the 60s – 80s [of the 20th century]. *Voprosy Istorii Estestvoznania i Tekhniki*, No. 4, pp. 55 – 65.

--- (2000, Russian), Pseudo-history and pseudo-mathematics. Phantasy in our life. *Uspekhi Matematich. Nauk* (translated as *Russ. Math. Surveys*), No. 2, vol. 55, pp. 159 – 161.

Ondar Kh. O. (1977, Russian), *Correspondence between A. A. Markov and A. A. Chuprov on the Theory of Probability and Mathematical Statistics*. New York, 1981. Based on archival sources but essentially corrupted by ignorance and indifference. Most mistakes left in translation.

Orwell G. (1945), *Animal Farm*. Many later editions by Penguin Books.

Pearson K. (1892), *Grammar of Science*. London. Many later editions and translations. Dover publ., 2004.

--- (1978), *History of Statistics in the 17th and 18th Centuries* etc. Lectures of 1921 – 1933. London. Editor E. S. Pearson.

Pfanzagl J., Sheynin O. (1996), A forerunner of the *t*-distribution. *Biometrika,* vol. 83, pp. 891 – 898.

--- (1997), Süssmilch. Incorporated in Kotz & Johnson (2006, vol. 13, pp. 8489 – 8496) but somehow published there anonymously.

Romanovsky V. I. (1938), *Matematicheskaia Statistika*. Moscow – Leningrad.

Segal S. L. (2003, 2004), *Mathematics under the Nazis*. Princeton – Oxford.

Shafarevich I. R. (2002), *Triekhtyshiacheletnia Zagadka* (Mystery Lasting Three Thousand Years). Moscow, 2006. Dirty anti-Semitic libel on the lowest level.

Sharon A. with Chanoff D. (1989), *Warrior*. New York.

Sheynin O. (1965, Russian), Adrain's work in the theory of errors. IMI, vol. 16, pp. 325 – 336. **S, G,** 1.

--- (1975), Kepler as a statistician. *Bull. Intern. Stat. Inst.*, vol. 46, pp. 341 – 354.

--- (1978), Theory of probability. In Kolmogorov & Youshkevich (1978/1992, 2001, pp. 211 – 288). Co-author B. V. Gnedenko.

--- (1990, Russian), *Aleksandr Chuprov. Life, Work, Correspondence*. Göttingen, 1996, 2011.

--- (1993, Russian), Markov's letters to the newspaper *Den*, 1914 – 1915. IMI, vol. 34, pp. 194 – 206. **S, G,** 85.

--- (1998a), Statistics in the Soviet epoch. *Jahrbücher f. Nationalökonomie u. Statistik*, Bd. 217, pp. 529 – 549.

--- (1998b), Statistical thinking in the *Bible* and the *Talmud*. *Annals of Science*, vol. 55, pp. 185 – 198.

--- (2001), Pirogov as a statistician. *Hist. Scientiarum*, vol. 10, pp. 213 – 225.

--- (2003a), Mises on mathematics in Nazi Germany. Ibidem, vol. 13, pp. 134 – 146.

--- (2003b), *Gumbel, Einstein and Russia*. Moscow. **S, G,** 12.

--- (2006a), Review of T. M. Porter, *K. Pearson*. Princeton, 2006. *Hist. Scientiarum*, vol. 16, pp. 206 – 209.

--- (2006b), Review of the translation of Jakob Bernoulli *Ars Conjectandi* by E. D. Sylla. Baltimore, 2006. Ibidem, pp. 212 – 214.

--- (2006c), Markov's work on the treatment of observations. Ibidem, vol. 16, pp. 80 – 95.

--- (2008a), Bortkiewicz' alleged discovery: the law of small numbers. Ibidem, vol. 18, pp. 36 – 48.

--- (2008b), Romanovsky's correspondence with K. Pearson and R. A. Fisher. *Archives d'hist. des sciences* No. 160 – 161, vol. 58, pp. 365 – 384.

--- (2017a), *Theory of Probability. Historical Essay*. Berlin. **S, G,** 10.

--- (2017b), *Black Book*. Berlin. **S, G,** 80.

Smit M. (1931), *Teoria i Praktika Sovetskoi Statistiki* (Theory and Practice of Soviet Statistics). Moscow. The edition of 1930 did not yet contain the Introduction with the quoted statement.

--- (1934, Russian), Against idealistic and mechanistic theories in the theory of Soviet statistics. *Planovoe Khoziastvo*, No. 7, pp. 217 – 231.

--- (1961), *Ocherki Istorii Bourgoisnoi Politicheskoi Ekonomii* (Essays on the History of the Bourgeois Political Economy). Moscow.

Solzhenitsyn A. I. (1974, Russian), *Archipelag Gulag*, vols. 1 – 3. Moscow, 1989. Many translations.

--- (2001 – 2002), *Dvesti Let Vmeste* (Two Hundred Years Together), vols 1 – 2. Moscow, 2013. Incomplete English translation in Internet.

Soveshchanie (1948), *Vtoroe Vsesoiuznoe Soveshchanie po Matematicheskoi Statistike* (Second All-Union Discussion on Math. Statistics). Tashkent.

Tikhomirov V. M. (2007, Russian), M. L. Liadov. IMI, vol. 12/47, pp. 132 – 147.

Tipolt A. N. (1972, Russian), From the history of the Demographic Institute. *Uchenye Zapiski po Statistike*, vol. 20, pp. 72 – 99.

Todhunter I. (1865), *History of Mathematical Theory of Probability*. New York, 1949, 1965.

Tutubalin V. N. (1972), *Teoriya Veroiyatnostei v Estestvoznanii* (Theory of Probability in Natural Science). Moscow. **S, G,** 45.

Voprosy (1961), *Obshchie Voprosy Primeneniya Matematiki v Ekonomike i Planirovanii* (General Issues of the Application of Mathematics in Economics and Planning). Moscow.

Youshkevich A. P., Rosenfeld B. A. (1996), Geometry. *Enc. Hist. Arabic Sci.*, vol. 2, pp. 447 – 494. London – New York.

Printed by Books on Demand GmbH, Norderstedt / Germany